P9-DCY-569

Thomas Paine's
Rights of Man

A Biography

Current and forthcoming titles in the
Books That Changed the World series:

Thomas Paine's
Rights of Man
A Biography

CHRISTOPHER HITCHENS

Grove Press
New York

Copyright © 2006 by Christopher Hitchens

All rights reserved. No part of this book may be reproduced in any form or by any electronic or mechanical means, or the facilitation thereof, including information storage and retrieval systems, without permission in writing from the publisher, except by a reviewer, who may quote brief passages in a review. Any members of educational institutions wishing to photocopy part or all of the work for classroom use, or publishers who would like to obtain permission to include the work in an anthology, should send their inquiries to Grove Atlantic, 154 West 14th Street, New York, NY 10011.

The author and publishers are grateful to Dwarf Music for permission to reproduce material from "As I Walked Out One Morning" copyright © 1968 by Dwarf Music. All rights reserved. International copyright secured.
Reprint by permission.

Printed in the United States of America

FIRST PAPERBACK EDITION

ISBN-13: 978-0-8021-4383-9
ISBN-10: 0-8021-4383-0

Design by Richard Marston

Grove Press
an imprint of Grove Atlantic
154 West 14th Street
New York, NY 10011

Distributed by Publishers Group West
groveatlantic.com

21 22 23 24 25   10 9 8 7 6 5

Dedicated by permission to President Jalal Talabani: first elected president of the Republic of Iraq; sworn foe of fascism and theocracy; leader of a national revolution and a people's army. In the hope that his long struggle will be successful, and will inspire emulation.

'Pain's wild rebellious burst proclaims her rights aloud...'

William Wordsworth: *Descriptive Sketches*

'As I walked out one morning, to breathe the air around Tom Paine's...'

Bob Dylan: 'As I Walked Out One Morning'

'To all these champions of the oppressed Paine set an example of courage, humanity and single-mindedness. When public issues were involved, he forgot personal prudence. The world decided, as it usually does in such cases, to punish him for his lack of self-seeking; to this day his fame is less than it would have been if his character had been less generous. Some worldly wisdom is required even to secure praise for the lack of it.'

Bertrand Russell: *The Fate of Thomas Paine*

CONTENTS

Children in the United States are taught early in life to sing 'My Country, 'tis of thee', in which the main verse goes:

> My Country, 'tis of thee
> Sweet land of liberty
> Of thee I sing
> Land where my fathers died
> Land of the Pilgrims' pride
> From every mountainside –
> Let freedom ring!

This is an averagely sentimental ditty, but it was promoted to immortality by the great Dr Martin Luther King, in the imperishable speech that he made on the steps of the Lincoln Memorial, at the climax of the civil rights 'March on Washington' in the spring of 1963. Seizing the familiar words of the schoolroom for his peroration, he demanded that freedom should ring from every hilltop, north and south, from New Hampshire to California and down to Mississippi, until the original promise of the United States had been kept for all its citizens. 'If America is to be a great nation,' he proclaimed, 'this must become true.'

'My Country, 'tis of thee' would be a fairly easy song for British schoolchildren to master as well. It is sung, for one thing, to the tune of the National Anthem. This rather unimaginative hymn – the first national anthem in the world, as it happens – seems to have originated as a Jacobite *chanson*, but was rewritten for the cause of (Protestant) Church and King in September 1745, as the Jacobite rebel invaders from Scotland were menacing the throne. A theatre audience in London rose to intone, as well as the first verse, the less commonly heard second one:

> O Lord our God arise,
> Scatter his enemies
> And make them fall:
> Confound their politics,
> Frustrate their knavish tricks
> On him our hopes are fix'd
> O save us all.

The 'him' in this case was George II, representative of the Hanoverian usurpation that endures on the British throne to the present day. By the early 1800s his son, George III, was being greeted by this song on official occasions. And by that time, another version was in circulation, written by the great radical artisan poet Joseph Mather:

God save great Thomas Paine,
His 'Rights of Man' explain
 To every soul.
He makes the blind to see
What dupes and slaves they be,
And points out liberty
 From pole to pole.

Thousands cry 'Church and King'
That well deserve to swing,
 All must allow:
Birmingham blush for shame,
Manchester do the same
Infamous is your name,
 Patriots vow.

Pull proud oppressors down,
Knock off each tyrant's crown,
 And break his sword;
Down aristocracy,
Set up democracy,
And from hypocrisy
 Save us good Lord.

Why should despotic pride
Usurp on every side?
 Let us be free:
Grant freedom's arms success,

And all her efforts bless,
Plant through the universe
    Liberty's Tree.

Facts are seditious things
When they touch courts and kings,
    Armies are raised,
Barracks and Bastilles built,
Innocence charged with guilt,
Blood most unjustly spilt,
    God stands amazed.

Despots may howl and yell,
Though they're in league with hell
    They'll not reign long;
Satan may lead the van,
And do the worst he can,
Paine and his 'Rights of Man'
    Shall be my song.

This fine parody, composed in 1791, is taught in no school and sung in no assembly. But it captures, with its defiant and satirical pugnacity, the spirit that was aroused that year by the publication of Thomas Paine's classic. Joseph Mather was a radical file-maker in the city of Sheffield; one wonders whether he inspired, or whether he drew from, the song that was struck up at an evening of the more mainstream Society for Constitutional Information, which at its London meeting in March 1791 voted its thanks to Paine and then heard members of the successful majority intone:

> God save The Rights of Man!
> Let despots, if they can,
> Them overthrow...

It seems likely that Mather was writing later in the year, since it is easy enough to interpret his apparently odd phrase 'Birmingham blush for shame'. It was in Birmingham in the autumn of 1791 that a Tory-inspired mob, frenzied by the cry of 'Church and King', broke into Joseph Priestley's house, destroying the library and laboratory of the self-taught scientist who had discovered oxygen. This incident – another of those historical episodes that is not taught in school – decided Priestley on a move to America, whose revolutionary and republican cause he had already espoused in a pamphlet. He was there to become a welcome guest, and a participant in the great Philadelphia renaissance that featured such men as Benjamin Franklin, Benjamin Rush and Thomas Jefferson. One should not allow oneself to forget that the English friends of the revolutions in America and France were not always greeted only with the high moral tones of Edmund Burke (who approved of the 'Church and King' mobocracy when the mob was on his side) but also with persecution and repression of quite a high and systematic degree.

Other contemporary clues can be found in Mather's lines. He used the word 'Patriot' to describe the supporters of the democratic and radical cause. This had also been the term employed by John Wilkes's faction in Parliament and its supporters outside it: the famous partisans of 'Wilkes and Liberty' against a German Crown and a Tory-dominated system of rotten boroughs. (It was only that version of 'Patriotism', incidentally, that the Tory Dr Samuel Johnson described, in a remark that has been misunderstood and mis-quoted ever since, as 'the last refuge of the scoundrel'.)

The word 'Bastille' was also fresh in the mind in 1791, as the symbol of the French absolutist monarchy and as a synonym for the many dark prisons in which the liberals of Europe had so long been confined and tortured. The Marquis de Lafayette, chivalric hero of both the American and the French Revolutions, gave the key of the Bastille to Thomas Paine and requested him to forward it to President George Washington as a token of French regard to the American people. Paine had done so with delight in the year before he published *Rights of Man*, adding a covering letter which described the key as 'this early trophy of the spoils of despot-ism, and the first ripe fruits of American principles trans-planted into Europe'. The key hangs to this day on the wall of Washington's home at Mount Vernon. The date of Paine's letter was the first of May, which a century or so later was the date selected by American workers as the one on which to begin the struggle for the eight-hour day, and afterwards by the labour movements of all countries as May Day: the holiday and carnival and fiesta of the oppressed.

Spring, and the natural world, were ordinary metaphors

for Paine, as they have always been for those who witness the melting of political glaciers and the unfreezing of the tundra of despotism. 'I have not the least doubt of the final and complete success of the French Revolution,' Paine went on in his letter to George Washington. 'Little ebbings and flowings, for and against, the natural companions of revolutions, sometimes appear, but the full current of it is, in my opinion, as fixed as the Gulf Stream.' The same metaphor, of a warming current coming from across the seas, is to be found in Paine's dedication of *Rights of Man*:

To

GEORGE WASHINGTON,

President of the United States of America

SIR,

I present you a small Treatise in defence of those Principles of Freedom which your exemplary Virtue hath so eminently contributed to establish. – That the Rights of Man may become as universal as your Benevolence can wish, and that you may enjoy the Happiness of seeing the New World regenerate the Old, is the Prayer of

SIR,

Your much obliged and

Obedient humble Servant,

THOMAS PAINE.[1]

It was that Pitt-supporting Tory, George Canning, who in 1826 claimed that he had 'called the New World into existence to redress the balance of the Old'. Winston Churchill, evoking the Atlantic alliance in a time of peril, told Parliament – this time quoting Arthur Hugh Clough – 'but westward look, the land is bright'. The metaphysical poets had often compared romantic America to a lover – 'my America, my new found land'. Pilgrims had sailed to 'the Americas' to establish doctrinal purity, and pirates had made the same voyage in search of treasure and slaves. In Paine's time, however, the New World of 'the United States of America' (a name he may have coined) was an actual and concrete achievement; not an imaginary Utopia but a home for liberty and the conscious first stage of a world revolution.

'Liberty's tree' would have been well understood by Mather's fellow artisans and self-taught workers, as the symbol of the Enlightenment and of democratic revolution. It recurs as an image in numberless poems, oaths, toasts and songs of the period, and from the United Irishmen all the way to the letters of Thomas Jefferson (who was not the only one to say that the tree of liberty must be nurtured by the blood of tyrants, as well as of patriots). The greeting of the radical Protestant-dominated United Irishmen went like this:

> 'Are you straight?'
> 'I am.'
> 'How straight?'
> 'As straight as a rush.'
> 'Go on, then.'
> 'In truth, in trust, in unity and liberty.'

'What have you got in your hand?'
'A green bough.'
'Where did it first grow?'
'In America.'
'Where did it bud?'
'In France.'
'Where are you going to plant it?'
'In the crown of Great Britain.'

Robert Burns wrote a poem called 'The Tree of Liberty', which opens in this vein:

Heard ye o' the tree o' France,
I watna what's the name o't;
Around it a' the patriots dance,
Weel Europe kens the fame o't.
It stands where once the Bastille stood,
A prison built by kings, man,
When Superstition's hellish brood
Kept France in leading-strings, man.

We can thus be sure that Burns – a great partisan of the 1789 Revolution in France – had read Thomas Paine's *Rights of Man*, which at one point described monarchy as a form which infantilized and retarded society as well as increased its tendency towards senility: 'It appears under all the characters of childhood, decrepitude, dotage, a thing at nurse, in leading strings, or on crutches.'[2] And Burns's most famous poem, 'For

a' that', breathes with a mighty scorn for the conceits of heredity and the hereditary principle, so comprehensively lam-
pooned by Paine. For their part, the United Irishmen,
founded in this epic year of 1791 to attach 'Protestants of the
middling ranks' to the cause of national and parliamentary
reform, made Paine an honorary member. He was one of
those rare Englishmen of the period who could write that:
'The suspicion that England governs Ireland for the purpose
of keeping her low, to prevent her becoming her rival in trade
and manufactures, will always operate to hold Ireland in a
state of sentimental hostility with England.'

To have had a hand in two revolutions, as Paine was later
to exult after his first adventures in France, was 'living to
some purpose'. That he was too optimistic is certain: both the
Revolutions of 1776 and 1789 were to disillusion him in
several ways. But his actual influence on revolutionary
change can be felt in many more than two countries, including the nation of his birth and its Irish and Scottish and Welsh
constituents.

The name of Paine will always be indissolubly linked to those
resonant words, the 'rights of man'. The book which bears
that noble title was, however, not just a paean to human
liberty. It was partly a short-term polemic, directed in particular at Edmund Burke's *Reflections on the Revolution in France*, a
very exceptional contribution to the energetic 'pamphlet
wars' that made the late eighteenth century, with its clubs and
pubs and coffee-houses and printshops, such an enlivening

period in Britain and France and America. It was also partly a revisionist history of England, written from the viewpoint of those who had gained the least from the Norman Conquest and the successive monarchical coups and usurpations. Then again it was a manifesto, setting out the basic principles of reform and, if necessary, of revolution. It did not disdain to put forward certain practical and immediate programmatic suggestions, designed to alleviate suffering and injustice in the here and now. But it always kept its sights raised to a point somewhat beyond the immediate political and social horizon. It is, in that sense, one of the first 'modern' texts. John Bunyan's *Pilgrim's Progress* may have kept alive the spirit of the English Revolution in countless poor and down-trodden homes, and the careful research of John Stuart Mill and others may have laid the basis for later Victorian social reform, but Thomas Paine's *Rights of Man* is both a trumpet of inspiration and a carefully wrought blueprint for a more rational and decent ordering of society, both domestically and on the international scene.

Indeed, it opens as a kind of one-man peace mission, devoted to the idea of warmer relations between Britain and France. Paine was a leading member of that British radical tradition that saw wars and armies as additional burdens on the people, and as reinforcements of existing autocracies. What better way for a ruling class to claim and hold power than to pose as the defenders of the nation? And what better way to keep unschooled and unemployed serfs in line than to give them the king's shilling and put them into uniform under aristocratic commanders? (The old folk expression, 'he's gone to the wars', or 'he's been in the wars', expresses by its plurality the vague fatalism about this, and the sense that every now and then it is expected that Johnnie will be marched off and perhaps, if God is merciful, will march back again.) Southey's *After Blenheim* catches this perfectly, as does Thackeray's *Barry Lyndon* and the fuddled old man in the alehouse in *Nineteen Eighty Four*, who blearily says to Winston Smith that 'It's all wars'.

Most of Britain's, or England's, martial and kingly battles had been either with France or in France, and Paine opened his Preface to *Rights of Man* with an account of a meeting he had had in 1787, two years before the fall of the Bastille, with some liberal-minded Frenchmen. Of one of these, the private secretary to an important minister, he reported finding:

That his sentiments and my own perfectly agreed with respect to the madness of war, and the wretched impolicy of two nations, like England and France, continually worrying each other, to no other end than that of a mutual increase of burdens and taxes. That I might be assured I had not misunderstood him, nor he me, I put the substance of our opinions into writing, and sent it to him; subjoining a request, that if I should see among the people of England, any disposition to cultivate a better understanding between the two nations than had hitherto prevailed, how far I might be authorized to say that the same disposition prevailed on the part of France? He answered me by letter in the most reserved manner, and that not for himself only, but for the Minister, with whose knowledge the letter was declared to be written.[3]

It takes a moment to appreciate the extraordinary impudence that this would have represented in its time. One can hear William Pitt's Tories growling and snarling – who is this upstart commoner who presumes to conduct his own diplomacy with Frenchmen? I myself cannot think of a precedent for it, but Paine was by then well used to executing unofficial missions of the diplomatic sort, on behalf of his newly adopted country, the United States of America. That same thought would have empurpled many Tories even more: whipper-snapper Paine acting on behalf of mutinous colonists to boot! However, it turns out that Paine was behaving more discreetly than many reactionaries might have supposed. He had sent his relevant Anglo-French correspondence to Edmund Burke, a trusty patriot and parliamentarian, whose defence of the American Revolution had won all-round respect. And yet, when the French rebellion had exploded on the world, Burke had hastened to the printer and had published one of the most sulphurous counter-revolutionary screeds of all time. It is important to understand, therefore, that *Rights of Man* has its private and emotional dimension: a note of plaintive disappointment from a former admirer that at times can sound almost like the tone of a despised lover.

The whole of Part One of the book, however, is an attempt as far as possible to avoid personalizing the question. In his stalwart advocacy of the revolution in France, Paine insists that it is Burke who has fallen into an emotional muddle. The persons and characters of King Louis and Marie Antoinette, upon whose behalf Burke expends such a great deal of outrage and misplaced gallantry, are irrelevant and Burke's prose a silly waste of feeling. The French people rebelled, not against these individual monarchs ('a mild and lawful monarch', as Burke rather amazingly described the then-tenant of Versailles) but against the whole *principle* of monarchy. They were punishing, not just the crimes of this incumbent, but the centuries of crime committed by the dynasty in whose name he ruled. Thus, in a sense, it could be argued that even poor Louis himself was a victim of the hereditary principle. This was not just a mere rhetorical stroke on Paine's part. In Boston and New York and Philadelphia, he well knew, portraits of King Louis were displayed in revolutionary homes as an *hommage* to the assistance rendered by France to the American rebellion.

In that struggle, nobody had been more to the fore than the dashing Marquis de Lafayette, whose forces had eventually compelled the surrender of King George's British and German invaders. Lafayette is nowadays somewhat in eclipse, despite the charming park opposite the White House that bears his name. But he actually played a part in *three* revolutions, those of 1776, 1789 and 1848, and was in his time the very talisman and emblem of daring and heroism. Later writers have clumsily compared Paine to Che Guevara as an internationalist, but for Paine himself the charisma belonged to nobody but Lafayette, whose title as 'Marquis' he was often reluctant, on republican grounds, to use in print. However, it obviously suited him to be able to deploy a member of the French nobility against the nostalgic Burke:

> M. de Lafayette went to America at an early period of the war, and continued a volunteer in her service to the end. His conduct through the whole of that enterprise is one of the most extraordinary that is to be found in the history of a young man, scarcely then twenty years of age. Situated in a country that was like the lap of sensual pleasure, and with the means of enjoying it, how few are there to be found who would exchange such a scene for the woods and wildernesses of America, and pass the flowery years of youth in unprofitable danger and hardship! but such is the fact. When the war ended, and he was on the point of taking his final departure, he presented himself to Congress, and contemplating, in his affectionate farewell, the revolution he had seen, expressed himself in these words: *'May this great monument, raised to Liberty, serve as a lesson to the oppressor and as an example to the oppressed!'* – When this address came to the hands of Dr Franklin, who was then in France, he applied to Count Vergennes to have it inserted in the French Gazette, but never could obtain his consent. The fact was, that Count Vergennes was an aristocratical despot at home, and dreaded the example of

the American revolution in France, as certain other persons
dread the example of the French revolution in England; and
Mr Burke's tribute of fear (for in this light his book must be
considered) runs parallel with Count Vergennes' refusal.[4]

The whole 'project' of *Rights of Man*, then, was in the first
instance an attempt to marry the ideas of the American and
French Revolutions, and in the second instance an attempt to
disseminate these ideas in Britain. For Paine, these objectives
were essentially three facets of the same symbol. For Burke,
they were radically incompatible. One reason for revisiting
both books, for any student who aspires to any sense of
history, is to see the same sequence of events debated by two
masterly contemporaries.

Burke believed that there already had been a revolution in
England, in 1688, and that it had settled the question for all
time. In his view, the 'Glorious Revolution' of that year had
instated a stable relationship between monarchy and people,
with everyone essentially knowing their place. Any further
interference with the machinery would be profane. It was
Paine's task to satirize this 'end of history' view, and to assert
that the right of the people to alter their government was
inherent and inalienable.

Paine was writing at a moment of hectic optimism when it
could be said that immediate questions were mainly relative,
and thus that the specific merits or vices of the sixteenth Louis
were negligible when one contemplated the historic imperative that 'the Augean stables of parasites and plunderers

[were] too abominably filthy to be cleansed, by anything short of a complete and universal revolution'. But he did not simply announce this as if any revolt, however bloody, would be better than none at all. He took particular care to note that, three days before the fall of the Bastille, Lafayette had asked the National Assembly to adopt a declaration of rights. It seemed as if, for the second time in a decade, a country would not just throw off monarchy but would also inscribe the inalienable rights of the citizen. But the words 'as if' are the ones to watch for. For the remainder of the first part of *Rights of Man*, Paine gave his own moment-by-moment version of the events that had made the overthrow of monarchy inescapable. It is a fascinating and often first-hand account, and most affecting to read because it was composed in a time of optimism.

Having dedicated his Part One to George Washington, one of the most conservative revolutionaries of all time (and a future target for his most bitter criticism), Paine dedicated Part Two – the less explicitly revolutionary half – to his more radical hero, Lafayette. He began with a few extra swipes at Burke, who had at one point undertaken to make a comparison of what he called the British constitution with the French one. He noted that Burke had not kept this promise, and also that he had further disdained any response to Part One.

This left the field clear for Paine to launch a spirited attack on the hereditary principle, which he ridiculed at length for its self-evident contradictions. To him, the idea of a hereditary ruler was as absurd as the idea of a hereditary mathematician, and put the country at the continual risk of being governed by an imbecile. (The madness of King George III lent extra point to these observations.)

Switching gears, he took up the implied challenge that is extended to all radicals, namely 'What would *you* do?' and made a series of detailed proposals for a future system of republican government. Some of these drew upon a comparison between the French system and the British one, and others were concerned with the state of the Treasury. Lampooning the finances of the Pitt ministry, Paine compared the combination of a small sinking fund with large borrowings to asking a man with a wooden leg to catch a hare: the longer they run, the further apart they grow. Finally, he adumbrated a very advanced plan for what we would now call a 'welfare state'. The response of Pitt's government was to try to arrest him for sedition. Paine was never to learn of what Pitt's niece, Lady Hester Stanhope, had reported. Her uncle, she said, 'used to say that Tom Paine was quite in the right, but then, he would add "what am I to do? As things are, if I were to encourage Tom Paine's opinions we should have a bloody revolution."' This oblique tribute from authority is proof in itself of the tremendous impact that was registered when one self-taught corset-maker and bridge-designer undertook to instruct his betters in the art of government, and based his audacious claim on the foundation of 'rights', a term which, once heard by its audience, it became impossible to make them forget.

CHAPTER 1

Paine in America

To begin with a summary of Paine's astonishing life and career is to commence with a sense of wonder that he was ever able to emerge at all. A favourite poem of the mid-eighteenth century was Thomas Gray's 'Elegy Written in a Country Churchyard', and I find it impossible to think about Paine without revisiting this masterpiece of the might-have-been:

> Perhaps in this neglected spot is laid
> Some heart once pregnant with celestial fire;
> Hands that the rod of empire might have sway'd,
> Or waked to ecstasy the living lyre:
>
> But Knowledge to their eyes her ample page
> Rich with the spoils of time did ne'er unroll;
> Chill Penury repress'd their noble rage,
> And froze the genial current of the soul.
>
> Full many a gem of purest ray serene,
> The dark unfathom'd caves of ocean bear:
> Full many a flower is born to blush unseen,
> And waste its sweetness on the desert air.

Some village-Hampden, that with dauntless breast
The little tyrant of his fields withstood;
Some mute inglorious Milton here may rest,
Some Cromwell, guiltless of his country's blood.

Gray, of course, does not omit to remind us that many latent absolutists and torturers have also gone to nameless dust without fulfilling their potential. His poem is not a work of mere sentiment. But when General Wolfe lay dying on the Plains of Abraham above Quebec in 1759, having defeated the French and having forever altered the destiny of the North American continent, he is supposed to have said that he would rather have composed Gray's *Elegy* than won this historic victory. That year, the son of Joseph and Frances Pain was just fifteen, and living a highly unpromising life in the bucolic town of Thetford, in deep East Anglia. Joseph was a corset-maker (a 'staymaker' in the idiom of the day) and a Quaker who had married the daughter of an Anglican lawyer. Young Thomas, sometimes known as Tom, did not add the 'e' to the family name until he emigrated to America in 1774. (I shall from now on follow the example of Professor A. J. Ayer and call him 'Thomas Paine' throughout.) But that was not the first time that he had run away.

Young Thomas's first bolt for freedom came at the age of sixteen, when he fled the confining apprenticeship to his father's staymaking business and made his way to the east coast of England, at Harwich, where he followed immemorial tradition by trying to go to sea. Later writers of stirring fiction for boys might have hesitated to invent a ship called *The Terrible*, commanded by a certain Captain Death, but such was the vessel, and such the master and commander, that might have carried this particular boy out of history. Joseph Pain arrived at the quayside in time to prevent his son's enlistment on the privateer, whether out of Quaker principle or because of a reluctance to part with an apprentice it is not known, and the lad returned to the indentures of corsetdom for another three years before heading seaward again in 1756. The Seven Years War between the British and French empires had begun, and this time he managed to get himself signed on, by Captain Mendez of the good ship *King of Prussia*. He lasted only a short time in this employment, seeing some action in the coastal and Channel waters and discovering that flying splinters could be as deadly as cannonballs, before evidently deciding that the war – which was eventually to precipitate revolution in both America and France – was not for him. He took his prize money – naval warfare at that date was still semi-piratical – and went to London to try and improve himself.

We cannot know for certain the fermentation that was at work within him, but there are three possible sources for it. The first was his upbringing. His father's Quakerism, for which Paine retained a lifelong respect, would have represented quite a strong form of dissent in the England of the day, and especially in a quasi-feudal town like Thetford, dominated by the Duke of Grafton. Quakers and other nonconformists kept alive another tradition – that of the English Revolution that had culminated in the execution of the impious King Charles I in 1649. At grammar school, Paine refused Latin lessons on his father's orders, Latin being the obscurantist official tongue of the throne and the popish altar. He concentrated instead on the English of Milton and Bunyan: the bards of the 'good old cause' of the Common-wealth. (One of Milton's most essential lines, 'By the known rules of ancient liberty', looked back to an innate freedom that predated kingship and nobility.)

A paradoxical reinforcement of this dissent came from compulsory Bible study at school, supplemented by instruction from Paine's Anglican mother. He was later to say that he found the teachings of Christianity, especially the human-sacrifice element in the story of the crucifixion, repellent from the start. Freethinking has good reason to be grateful to Mrs Pain for her efforts.

A second influence may have been the time that Paine spent on the lower deck of the *King of Prussia*. As Patrick O'Brian's remarkable seafaring novels remind us, the crews of the Royal Navy were full of nonconformist enthusiasts, who may have fought for the Crown at sea but who were Levellers and Republicans on land. Third – and much better documented – we can trace the influence of the London scene. A new class of literate artisans was making its appearance, much influenced by the thirst for knowledge and by the scien-tific innovations of the period. Paine became a habitué of the working-man's lecture hall and the freethinker's tavern, where enthusiastic discussion groups were the yeast for self-improvement and political reform.

This didn't give Paine a living, however, and the next few years of his life remind one of Saul Bellow's Augie March, for whom the laconic term 'various jobs' provided the 'Rosetta Stone' of his life. In 1758 he moved to the Channel port of Sandwich and became a staymaker after all. There he attended Wesleyan meetings and took part in the zealous Methodist promotion of 'good works' and charity. He met and married a serving girl named Mary Lambert, daughter of an Excise officer or Customs official, but in 1760 she died, with her baby, in childbirth. It was back to Thetford for Paine, where with some help from the local Grafton magnates he sat the examination to become an Excise officer himself. By 1764 he had been given a post of responsibility on the North Sea coast, stamping goods for duty and watching for smugglers. He suffered dismissal after a year or so, having allegedly stamped some bales without properly inspecting them. This reverse sent him back to London to petition the Commissioners of the Excise for reinstatement. This was granted after he submitted a grovelling letter; it was evident that he was not suspected of having taken any bribe. But reinstatement did not mean immediate reappointment, and for a while Paine had to subsist on what he could get for teaching poor children. This second period in London was to be decisive in his life, however, because he renewed acquaintance with one of his old lecturers, the painter and astronomer James Ferguson, and through him was introduced to Benjamin Franklin, a man who personified the alliance between scientific inquiry and free thought.

Exigency still drove Paine and, although he had the nerve
to decline the next offer he had from the Excise – a post in a
remote part of Cornwall – in 1768 he finally accepted a position at the Customs house in the Sussex town of Lewes, on the
south coast. Here, he began to emerge as a figure in his own
right. The town was small but like many seaports it had an
open mind, and the radical tradition was deep-rooted there.
At the White Hart tavern, Paine became a notable member of
the Headstrong Club, which combined spirited dining with
spirited debating, and also of the local council. He took lodgings with Samuel Ollive, a well-liked local tobacconist, and on
his death in 1769 succeeded to proprietorship of the business.
Two years later, he married the old man's daughter,
Elizabeth. He might, if the marriage had lasted, have become
a well-found and humorous Whig: a red-faced local 'character', fond of a drop of brandy, with a fund of anecdote and a
reputation as a bit of a rebel.

Instead, he literally talked his way out of such a fate. When
the Excise men of the south coast decided to protest at their
abysmal wage and to seek redress from Parliament, they
bethought themselves of the eloquent debater and sometime
lay-preacher Thomas Paine, and invited him to be their advocate and spokesman. He agreed to write the Excise men's petition, and to travel to London to lobby for their cause. He was
then kept hanging about in many an establishment anteroom
over the winter of 1772–3, and victimized for his pertinacity
by receiving yet another notice of dismissal from the Excise
Commission. Meanwhile, the tobacco shop in Lewes failed in

his absence, and his marriage expired in circumstances that are not clear. Paine was no ladies' man, we know, and he acted with a generosity to his wife that may have indicated an urgent desire to be gone. He settled up in Lewes, went back to London, and presented himself to Benjamin Franklin.

This distinguished gentleman, who had been in London as a representative of the American colonies, had recently had his own patriotism sorely tested. Attempting to redress some of the more obvious injustices of Britain's rule over the thirteen colonies, he had been very roughly handled at committee hearings in Parliament and accused, in effect, of being a subversive. The long stupidity of King George's policy could have been designed to make English Americans into revolutionaries, though it had not yet had quite that effect. Franklin – the discoverer of the lightning-rod, and of the connection between lightning and electricity – gave Paine advice that could be summarized in the later slogan, 'Go West, Young Man'. Franklin went further, and equipped him with a letter of introduction to his son William, who was then the Governor of New Jersey, and to his son-in-law Richard Bache, an underwriter in Philadelphia. It read:

> The bearer Mr Thomas Pain is very well recommended to me as an ingenious worthy young man. He goes to Pennsylvania with a view of settling there. I request you to give him your best advice and countenance, as he is quite a stranger there. If you can put him in a way of obtaining employment as a clerk, or assistant tutor in a school, or

assistant surveyor (in all of which I think him very capable,)
so that he may procure a subsistence at least, till he can make
acquaintance and obtain a knowledge of the country, you
will do well, and much oblige your affectionate father.[1]

That was a slightly tepid recommendation, perhaps –
Franklin's acquaintance with the young man was not a long
or a deep one – but it was enough. In September 1774 Paine
took ship for Philadelphia. Once again, he was almost lost to
history by an outbreak of either typhus or scurvy on board,
and had to be carried ashore on a stretcher. This was a shaky
start to an immense redress in the New World, this time one
imported from the Old.

For the first time in his life, Paine was in exactly the right
place at exactly the right time. Philadelphia was the capital of
a state – Pennsylvania – that had been founded by the Quaker
William Penn. It was hospitable to every form of religious and
political dissent, and as we have seen from the example of
Priestley, Franklin and others, a magnet city for those who
wished to pursue scientific inquiry. It boasted several excellent bookstores and contained many tavern-based discussion
groups where a veteran of the White Hart at Lewes could
prove himself. Paine had hardly begun his acquaintance with
this exciting town when he met Robert Aitken, a bookstore
proprietor who was hoping to start a new publication, *The
Pennsylvania Journal*. He almost at once invited Paine to take
on the managing editorship. In the first issue, Paine proved
himself a natural journalist by writing an editorial which

managed to extract good copy from his awful experience on the Atlantic crossing:

> Degeneracy here is almost a useless word. Those who are conversant with Europe would be tempted to believe that even the air of the Atlantic disagrees with the constitution of foreign vices; if they survive the voyage, they either expire on their arrival, or linger away in an incurable consumption. There is a happy something which disarms them of all their power both of infection and attraction.[2]

I have not been able to discover whether Paine was writing this in conscious opposition to the most illustrious European natural scientist of his day, the Comte de Buffon, who stoutly maintained that the very atmosphere of America was conducive to cretinism in man and beast. (Thomas Jefferson, then unknown to Paine, was to compose his *Notes on the State of Virginia* partly as a reply to Buffon's theories.) At any rate, he approached his new country with all the zeal of a new convert and enthusiast.

By the time of Paine's disembarkation, the colonial crisis in relations with the British motherland was already mounting. In order to pay for the expenses of the Seven Years War, which had removed the French military presence, London had imposed new taxes on the supposedly grateful colonies, and had furthermore decided to use these colonies as a dumping-ground for surplus products from elsewhere in the Empire – most famously the tea of the East India Company. In most minds, this was still a quarrel within the family. Men like Samuel Adams in Boston, Thomas Jefferson in Virginia and Benjamin Franklin, shuttling between London and Pennsylvania, were committed to protecting their rights as freeborn Englishmen under the Crown. But Crown policy, like a brittle antique sword, was dull and inflexible, and insisted upon taxation without representation.

Throughout 1775, Paine used a number of pseudonyms – 'Atlanticus' and 'Amicus' – to produce a stream of articles. By no means starry-eyed about his new homeland, he was swift in his denunciation of the slave trade, which maintained an open market in human beings in Philadelphia itself. 'That some desperate wretches should be willing to steal and enslave men by violence and murder for gain, is rather lamentable than strange. But that many civilized, nay, Christianized people should approve, and be concerned in the savage practice, is surprising.'[3] He announced himself an abolitionist, and became a founding member of the American Anti-Slavery Society. He also found the time to reflect upon a system of welfare for the young, and pensions for the old, that was unique for its time and which will recur as the story proceeds.

In April 1775 a small but deep trench of blood was filled, between British and American forces, at the battles of Lexington and Concord. From this point onwards, the dispute between Crown and colonists ceased to be fraternal and became fratricidal. Paine was readier than most to advocate separation and independence: his own experience of being 'English' had not been that of a gentleman farmer or

protected tradesman, but rather that of an ill-used civil
servant. By September he had published a song entitled –
what else? – 'The Liberty Tree'. Greatly inferior to the work of
Joseph Mather, its concluding verse went:

> But hear, O ye swains ('tis a tale most profane),
> How all the tyrannical powers,
> King, Commons and Lords, are uniting amain
> To cut down this guardian of ours.
> From the East to the West blow the trumpet to arms,
> Thro' the land let the sound of it flee:
> Let the far and the near all unite with a cheer,
> In defense of our Liberty Tree.[4]

He began to speak openly of independence, taking care to
phrase his convictions in quasi-biblical tones. 'Call it independence or what you will,' he wrote, 'if it is the cause of God
and humanity it will go on. And when the Almighty shall
have blest us, and made us a people dependent only on him,
then may our first gratitude be shown by an act of continental
legislation, which shall put a stop to the importation of
Negroes for sale, soften the hard fate of those already here,
and in time procure their freedom.' ('Continental' was the
rather grand name that the colonists had given to their
Congress, with its thirteen state delegations. At the time,
America was to the northern continent rather what Chile is to
the southern one – a long ribbon of territory extending down
the littoral of an ocean, and hemmed in by mountains on the

landward side. But there was a latent ambition to add at least British Canada to the tally of independent states, as well as to expand into the interior.)

Simultaneously, Paine repudiated the absolutism of Quakers in respect of the use of force. Repudiation of arms was all very well, 'but unless the whole will, the matter ends, and I take up my musket and thank heaven he has put it in my power'.[5] And he criticized those who looked only to the interests of their own particular colony, insisting that people should start thinking of themselves as 'Americans'.

In retrospect, all things seem to have pressed towards the event. But while a rebellion over colonial grievance was almost certainly inevitable, a 'war of independence' was not. Paine had been honing his quill on the question for some time. He was fortuitously separated from his post at the *Pennsylvania Magazine* in late 1775, having had a falling out with one of its sponsors (who in revenge spread the rumour that Paine was a heavy drinker, a slur that clung to him throughout his life, most probably because it was partly true). He was now in every sense 'free' to unmask his batteries, and to produce the largest achievement in the history of pamphleteering. Of *Common Sense* it can be said, without any risk of cliché, that it was a catalyst that altered the course of history.

The catalyst of the catalyst may well have been Dr Benjamin Rush, a brilliant Philadelphia physician who held strong abolitionist views and took an active part in scientific and rationalist discussions in the city. He urged Paine to write a polemical summary of the American case, in order to rally the public, but to avoid the dread words 'independence' and 'republicanism'. Paine was not naturally contra-suggestible, but we may nevertheless thank Dr Rush for helping him to make up his mind. He determined to call for separation from Britain, and furthermore to call for a new form of government.

There is no official memorial to Thomas Paine, the unofficial 'founding father', in Washington. None the less, most young Americans at some time or another are told to read his *Common Sense*, and his later pamphlet *The Crisis*, and some of the phrases from both are part of the common stock of political and journalistic discourse. It is not difficult, even at this remove, to understand why such a terse and concentrated work should have had the effect that it did.

Paine first appealed to the natural pride of Americans as hard-working pioneers who had laboured manfully to create a new society. 'Society,' he said, antedated all forms of government, which was superimposed upon it as, at best, a necessary evil. He then spoke to them in the tones of the only book they all had in common, namely the Christian Bible (albeit in its 'King James' English version). He sought to demonstrate that the Old Testament contained no warrant for kingship, while managing to imply, flatteringly, that the original non-hierarchical Eden had been replicated in the New World. He did not, of course, trouble himself with those passages of scripture which do suggest that the powers that be are ordained of God. With a similar disregard for paradox and contradiction, he founded many of his claims of ancient

liberty on the ancestral rights of Englishmen to be free of conquest and usurpation by foreign monarchs, such as William
the Conqueror, and quoted Milton just as any Cromwellian
partisan might have done. Yet he took particular care to stress
that many of the colonists were not English, and thus that the
demand of allegiance to a British Crown was essentially non-
binding on them. Prefiguring the idea of a multi-ethnic state,
he asserted that:

> This new world hath been the asylum for the persecuted
> lovers of civil and religious liberty from *every part* of
> Europe… all Europeans meeting in America, or any other
> quarter of the globe, are *countrymen;* for England, Holland,
> Germany, or Sweden, when compared with the whole, stand
> in the same places on the larger scale, which the divisions of
> street, town and county do on the smaller ones; distinctions
> too limited for continental minds. Not one third of the inhab-
> itants, even of this province, are of English descent.[6]

This alone was enough to dismiss the sentimental idea of
Britain as the parent or 'mother' country: a lazy phrase then in
common use.

To this, Paine also added the idea of religious diversity.
Despite the presence of several versions of Christian belief on
American soil, the Church of England still demanded, as it
did at home, a subsidy from the state and a monopoly on
orthodoxy. This 'Episcopalian' arrogance revolted Paine, who

wrote that the government should have no role save that of the guarantor of confessional pluralism.

Perhaps most nobly of all, he reacted with disgust to the British policy of divide-and-rule, which offered inducements to American Indians and freed slaves if they would join the ranks of King George's army. This, wrote Paine, was doing two sorts of injustice, both to the earlier victims of British policy and to the more recent targets of it: 'the cruelty hath a double guilt, it is dealing brutally by us, and treacherously by them.' All these moral strokes, however, and all these successful and amusing lampoons upon the absurd crowned figure of King George III and his marauding monarchical predecessors, were not enough in themselves. Paine tipped the balance, in the mind of his readers, by insisting on two very practical points. Since separation was inescapable sooner or later, might not NOW be the time? And was it not the case that Americans were already strong and capable enough to do it?

To these two positive propositions he added a third and an admonitory one. It was understandable that peaceful and prosperous citizens should fear war and disorder. Yet did not the British connection allow London to declare war, at any time, on behalf of all its imperial subjects? 'Europe is too thickly planted with kingdoms to be long at peace, and whenever a war breaks out between England and any foreign power, the trade of America goes to ruin, because of *her connection with England*.' In a later poem written against the American colonists, and sneering at them for their stab-in-the-back opportunism, Rudyard Kipling was to write:

'Twas not while England's sword unsheathed
Put half a world to flight,
Nor while their new-built cities breathed
Secure behind her might
Not while she poured from Pole to Line
Treasure and ships and men –
These worshippers at Freedom's shrine,
They did not quit her then!

Not till their foes were driven forth
By England o'er the main –
Not till the Frenchman from the North
Had gone with shattered Spain;
Not till the clean-swept oceans showed
No hostile flag unrolled
Did they remember what they owed
To Freedom – and were bold![7]

Even the title of this poem, 'The American Rebellion (1776)'
was condescending. But the ability of George III to enlist
America in Britain's war, and furthermore to unload German
troops and Indian tea on American soil, was decisive in
helping make Paine's case for him. (Kipling's beloved India
was later to demand independence partly because, in both
1914 and 1939, London had without notice or consultation
declared war on India's behalf.)

As Paine went on to say, blood had already been spilled
at Bunker Hill and elsewhere, and was this sacrifice to be

dedicated to the mere paltry aim of repealing a few taxes and duties? Replying to those who felt that they were not strong enough to fight the British Empire, Paine employed more practical reasoning, providing charts that showed how easily Americans could build their own army and navy (and predicting that one day America would outperform the world in shipbuilding).

Catching a mood that was rapidly spreading in any case, he challenged those who largely agreed but who hesitantly asked if this was quite the right time. That, he said, was not really the question. 'The inquiry ceases at once, for, *the time hath found us.*' By slow degrees, punctuated with real flashes of rhetoric, he assembled an argument that could be summarized as *carpe diem*, or 'seize the day'. Quoting another author, he reminded his readers that 'The science of the politician consists in fixing the true point of happiness and freedom. Those men would deserve the gratitude of ages, who should discover a mode of government that contained the greatest sum of individual happiness, with the least national expense.' Shamelessly appealing to the religious faith – especially the Protestantism – of his audience, and answering those who wondered where the king of America would come from, he retorted: 'I'll tell you Friend, he reigns above, and doth not make havoc of mankind like the Royal Brute of Britain.' Loud cheers for that. In this invocation of 'happiness', and bill of indictment against King George, and in his call for the publication of a 'manifesto' to inform the world of American claims and grievances, Paine directly anticipates Thomas Jefferson's wording of the later Declaration of Independence, with its 'pursuit of happiness', its itemization of a 'long train of abuses and usurpations', and its 'decent respect to the opinions of mankind'. Indeed – and this time slightly reverting to the English tradition that he had elsewhere depicted as non-binding – Paine even prefigured the future American Constitution in his call for a charter, based on Magna Carta, that would codify rights, set up a representative Congress and establish a permanent connection between the future 'United States of America'. This seems to be the first time that the phrase was actually used.

Paine argued from nature, as the first source of human and natural right. He analogized nature, saying that this was the 'seed time' and that it would be folly to miss it. He also argued that the natural order favoured independence, in that it was absurd for a continent to be governed by an island. He even hinted at a special providence: 'The Reformation was preceded by the discovery of America: As if the Almighty graciously meant to open a sanctuary to the persecuted in future years.' Writing many decades before Emma Lazarus composed the lines incised on the Statue of Liberty, he appealed:

> O ye that love mankind! Ye that dare oppose, not only the tyranny but the tyrant, stand forth! Every spot of the old world is overrun with oppression. Freedom hath been hunted round the globe. Asia, and Africa have long expelled her. – Europe regards her like a stranger, and England hath

given her warning to depart. O! Receive the fugitive, and
prepare in time an asylum for mankind.[8]

The entire appeal was published, in just under fifty pages,
on 10 January 1776. Dr Rush, who had suggested the title, also
found Paine a printer. The result was a bestseller on a scale
hitherto unknown and, according to Paine's biographer
Harvey Kaye, not since surpassed. It has been estimated that,
with pirate editions, *Common Sense* sold half a million copies
in the course of the Revolution. An edition was printed in
German, versions were reprinted in newspapers. Literacy
was by no means universal, though it was on the rise among
the radical and artisan classes, and very often the pamphlet
was read aloud, among families or in taverns. With near-
perfect pitch, Paine had caught the tone of voice that many
people actually used, while yoking this earthy appeal
(demotic jokes at the expense of monarchy) to a style that rose
to the inspirational. It was a nice combination of the lay
preacher with the rationalist and it was, in dress rehearsal, an
assumption of claim by the rights of man.

There was considerable speculation about the author-
ship, and considerable unease as well among the more conservative element. John Adams, in particular, detested its
subversive tone and its implicit elevation of the common
herd. (The later quarrels between Adams and Jefferson,
which marked the early years of the republic and supplied
the benchmarks for all future 'left' versus 'right' disputes in
American politics, were always, either openly or covertly,

arguments about Thomas Paine.) But within a few months, the Continental Congress had decided on an irrevocable Declaration of Independence and appointed a committee, which included Adams, Jefferson and Franklin, to draft it. It was Jefferson who was nominated to pull the threads together in one version, and it is obvious that he had both read and approved of *Common Sense*. (He even inserted a paragraph denouncing the slave trade, which was cut out by the Congress before the document was approved and published.)

Common Sense was signed by 'an Englishman'. Paine's next essay was to be signed with the pseudonym, or rather *nom de guerre*, 'Common Sense'. This next piece was *The Crisis*, which, perhaps to avoid identification with a pro-Revolution sheet in pre-1776 London, was sometimes reprinted under the title 'The American Crisis'. It was written at a time when Paine's prediction of a relatively easy victory over the British had conspicuously failed to come true. The winter following the Declaration had seen a series of defeats for George Washington's amateur army, with the loss of New York, the abandonment by Congress of Philadelphia, and an ignominious retreat across New Jersey. Paine had shouldered a musket and become attached as an aide to General Nathanael Greene, and had seen the rout at first hand. Determined to rally the flagging volunteers and instil morale by the recruitment of fresh ones, he wrote one of the greatest campfire and eve-of-battle orations since Agincourt:

These are the times that try men's souls: The summer soldier
and the sunshine patriot will, in this crisis, shrink from the
service of his country, but he that stands it NOW, deserves
the love and thanks of man and woman. Tyranny, like hell,
is not easily conquered; yet we have this consolation with us,
that the harder the conflict the more glorious the triumph.
What we obtain too cheap, we esteem too lightly – 'Tis
dearness only that gives everything its value.[9]

Paine had studied Shakespeare at Thetford and conceiv-
ably, despite his lack of respect for kingship, he remembered
Henry's V reply to the French herald: 'We would not seek a
battle as we are; nor, as we are, we say we would not shun it.'
He certainly heaped praise on those who would, one day, be
proud of never having deserted. But his chief concern was to
swell the ranks, and he asked for leave on his own behalf in
order to have the address printed as a pamphlet. Once again
the reception and sale were extraordinary, and had the effect
of bringing more men to Washington's colours. Before the
battle of Trenton, during which a daring night-time attack
surprised Britain's German mercenaries while they were
having a Christmas carouse, Washington ordered *The Crisis* to
be read to the assembled soldiers. I have a personal favourite
among its passages, which might not have struck the yeoman
soldiers in quite the same way:

I once felt all that kind of anger, which a man ought to feel,
against the mean principles that are held by the Tories: A

noted one, who kept a tavern at Amboy, was standing at
his door, with as pretty a child in his hand, about eight or
nine years old, as most I ever saw, and after speaking his
mind as freely as he thought was prudent, finished with
this unfatherly expression, 'Well, *give me peace in my day.*'
Not a man lives on the Continent but fully believes that a
separation must some time or another finally take place,
and a generous parent would have said, '*If there must be
trouble, let it be in my day, that my child may have peace;*' and
this single reflection, well applied, is sufficient to wake
every man to duty.[10]

This is curious and touching and it will, as we proceed, prove
interesting. It was not only Neville Chamberlain, fawning on
Adolf Hitler at Munich in 1938, who gave 'Toryism' a bad
name for all eternity by his wish-fulfilment pretence of 'peace
in our time'. Most pacifists and anti-warriors also invoke the
sacrifice of their living descendants on the battlefield as a
reason to avoid, or perhaps only to postpone, war. The child-
less Paine deftly avoids this difficulty by instancing an infant,
of unspecified gender, who is well below military age, and
who can thereby advance the claims of posterity. But this
would eventually tell against his other belief that no one generation can, by right, determine the destiny of another.

Paine continued to produce a series of *Crisis* papers
throughout the remainder of the revolutionary war. These are
of mainly immediate interest: they taunt and goad Lord
Howe, the British commander, and they mock the pretensions

of monarchy and aristocracy. Perhaps slightly too often, Paine stressed the danger of rape at the hands of the Hessian troops, and urged American men to defend the chastity of their young women. Occasionally he showed some of his old Methodist fire, anticipating Clough's 'Say not the struggle naught availeth' by writing: 'Say not that thousands are gone, turn out your tens of thousands; throw not the burden of the day upon Providence but *"show your faith by your works"*, that God may bless you.'[11] He made a blistering attack on the leadership of the Quakers, who had gone beyond mere pacifism by announcing their allegiance to the British. And he sarcastically instructed Lord Howe in the pitfalls of what would come to be known as guerrilla warfare:

> By what means, may I ask, do you expect to conquer
> America? If you could not effect it in the summer when our
> army was less than yours, nor in the winter when we had
> none, how are you to do it? In point of generalship you have
> been outwitted, and in point of fortitude outdone; your
> advantages turn out to be your loss, and show us that it is in
> our power to ruin you by gifts: Like a game of drafts we can
> move out of *one* square to let you come in, in order that we
> may afterwards take two or three for one; and as we can
> always keep a double corner for ourselves, we can always
> prevent a total defeat. You cannot be so insensible as not to
> see that we have two to one the advantage of you, because
> we conquer by a drawn game, and you lose by it.[12]

In the result, the British were finally cut off and surrounded at Yorktown in October 1781, and compelled to surrender by the counterweight supplied by French ships and soldiers, including the legendary volunteer Lafayette. Paine had been a member of the delegation that visited Paris to solicit the aid. (This revenge, on the part of France, for her defeat in the Seven Years War, was to have momentous consequences. The expense of the French expedition provoked a crisis in the domestic exchequer, which was to lead Louis XVI to convene a fateful meeting of the Estates General.)

War in continental America had had a less debilitating effect. There was considerably more social solidarity, and greatly increased identification with the new country. During the struggle, Paine had urged the wealthy to contribute their share for defence, and had set an example by foregoing royalties on his pamphlets and by making a donation from his own small funds. This levelling tendency on his part made him some vicious enemies among the traditional elite, such as Gouverneur Morris and John Adams, and though George Washington urged a public vote of money to Paine in compensation for his many voluntary services, there were those who saw to it that the payment was either reduced or held up. He did, however, receive a farm and a house, confiscated from a fleeing Tory, from the grateful state of New York.

Politics and military affairs had claimed most of his time since he landed in Philadelphia, but Paine had always wanted to contribute something in the field of science and innovation. For many years, he had nurtured the idea of an iron bridge, long and strong enough to span a major river. This was a typical 'Enlightenment' project, employing new methods of engineering to lighten the human load and to enhance contact between distant places. (Bridges, one might say, are progressive by definition and, since there is no such thing as a one-way bridge, they are also dialectical and reciprocal.) Like many inventors and innovators, Paine lacked capital. He determined to seek it, and the setting for his bridge, back in Europe. And it may be that, as Che Guevara once put it, he could feel Rosinante's bony ribs once again creaking between his legs.

Madame Roland, who was later to become a friend of Paine's in the course of the French Revolution, pronounced that she found him 'more fit, as it were, to scatter the kindling sparks than to lay the foundation or prepare the formation of a government. Paine is better at lighting the way for revolution than drafting a constitution... or the day-to-day work of a legislator.' She seconded a judgement that was made by many, about Paine's essential quixotry. (We recall how Guevara chafed at having to run the National Bank of Cuba, which he did so badly, when he could have been out in the mountains of Bolivia raising a revolt, at which he failed even worse.)

In point of fact, Paine was by no means a failure when it came to practical and mundane matters. His works were always full of statistical tables and other actuarial labour, laying out a feasible basis for this or that reform or expenditure. Before he left the United States for Europe once more, he acted as secretary to the Pennsylvania legislature, helping to draft at least one piece of legislation – the abolition of the trade in slaves – which was dear to him. He also wrote a number of articles urging the need for a serious and permanent machinery for resolving differences between the states. These were ostensibly tedious and provincial disputes, about the allocation of territorial boundaries and the discrepancies in contributions to the federal budget, but he correctly saw that they had large implications and he would have made an interesting participant in the great debate at Philadelphia, in 1788, which eventually evolved into the main architecture of the United States Constitution. But by then, Paine had recrossed the Atlantic.

Before he departed, he did write one essay that gave a clue to his state of mind, and could to some extent license the view of Madame Roland. The Abbé Raynal, otherwise known as Guillaume Raynal, had written a book entitled *Révolution d'Amerique*. In this volume, this rebel priest had sought to minimize the importance of 1776, advancing the rather reductionist and economist view that no greater principle had been involved than a taxpayers' revolt, of the sort that was commonplace in history. He referred to the precipitating events, slightingly, as 'a slight tax upon the colonies'. This would be, perhaps, in Christian terms, not unlike weighing and valuing the thirty pieces of silver. The Abbé may have been correct in certain narrative respects: there had indeed been a moment in 1778 when the Congress agreed to consider a British offer of compromise on the taxes. But Paine held a loftier view of matters in general, and took issue with Raynal on the limited character of the revolution. It was by no means, he insisted, the product of a petty local and fiscal quarrel. It was, rather, a universal promulgation of inalienable rights:

> A union so extensive, continued and determined, suffering with patience and never in despair, could not have been pro-duced by common [i.e. banal] causes. It must be something capable of reaching the whole soul of man and arming it with perpetual energy. It is in vain to look for precedents among the revolutions of former ages... The spring, the progress, the object, the consequences, nay, the men, their habits of thinking, and all the circumstances of the country, are different.[13]

This was, obviously, to have it both ways, if not indeed three ways. Paine had excellent personal reasons to know that there had indeed been moments of 'despair' during the American revolutionary war: if it had been otherwise he would not have needed to keep churning out the *Crisis* papers. Furthermore, either Americans were exceptional, as his last sentence above seems to suggest, or they were not. On the general applicability of the lessons, however, he was unwavering. 'The true idea of a great nation is that which pro-motes and extends the principles of universal society.' In 1782, when Paine published this open *Letter to the Abbé Raynal*, the time was not far off when the imposing clerical establish-ment in France was to find this out for itself, and in the hardest way. When Paine made his way back to Europe, he was one of those slender reeds that contain the flame stolen so audaciously by Prometheus from the gods themselves.

CHAPTER 2

Paine in Europe

On the return voyage to Europe, Paine was once again following the advice of Benjamin Franklin, who had told him that – especially once he had got himself on the wrong side of a bitter argument about the viability of a bank in Philadelphia – he would do well to seek sponsors for his bridge in either Paris or London. He chose the month of April 1787 to depart, and arrived at a time when Europe was pregnant with revolutionary and radical promise.

In Paris, he did not lack for well-placed friends. His admirer Thomas Jefferson had been appointed to be American Minister to France. The Marquis de Lafayette, wreathed with American laurels, was also at his disposal. Men of learning and wit were coming to the fore, and 'reason' was the watchword. The prestige of anyone coming from America was high: Lafayette kept a copy of the American Declaration on one panel of his study, leaving the opposite panel undecorated until the happy day when it should be adorned by a similar French one. Many eminent Parisians expressed interest in the design and scope of Paine's iron bridge – this being still a wooden age in many respects – though none would absolutely commit themselves.

Across the Channel, and in pursuit of the same goal, Paine took up one of the most improbable friendships – or so at least it must seem to us in retrospect – that there has ever been. On more than one of his trips into the country, to scout a possible location for the bridge, he was in company with Edmund Burke. He appears to have been Burke's guest, and to have enjoyed his conversation. 'We hunt in pairs,' as Burke himself put it. At that moment, there would have seemed no reason for enmity. To the contrary, if anything. Burke had published, in 1770, his *Thoughts on the Causes of the Present Discontents*. This had argued that it was corrupt and arbitrary authority, and not the revulsion against it, that required justification. He had waged an extraordinary campaign in Parliament for the impeachment of Warren Hastings, and denounced the hideous depredations of the East India Company against the exploited and humiliated peoples of India. His 'Sketch of a Negro Code', written in the early 1780s, had marked him out as an advanced critic of the slave trade. He had opposed the proposal for the seating of American slaveholders at Westminster and had been, in his capacity as lobbyist for the colony of New York, a strong defender of the violated rights of the American colonists. He was a man, furthermore, of large personality and wide learning. We need not take the Tory Dr Johnson's word – given as it was on several occasions – for this. William Hazlitt, one of the firebrands of the radical movement of the period, announced that 'It has always been with me, a test of the sense and candour of anyone belonging to the opposite party, whether he allowed Burke to be a great man.'[1] There is no reason to think that Paine did not share this view. Indeed, it is obvious from the shock he expressed, at the tone of Burke's *Reflections on the Revolution in France*, that he felt like a friend betrayed.

I am going to postpone a full discussion of the dispute between Burke and Paine to the next chapter. The French Revolution, which split British politics in several directions, at first struck Paine as a natural extension of the American one: the perfect refutation in practice of the narrow-minded Abbé Raynal. Paine's old friend, the Marquis de Lafayette, who had been very prominent in the parliamentary exchanges that led to the gradual isolation of the French ruling dynasty, was also the commander of the National Guard and very much in the thick of the inspiring street demonstrations that had culminated in the fall of the Bastille. Thomas Jefferson was likewise a deeply involved participant in the meetings of Parisian intellectuals, and helped to draft the first *Déclaration des Droits de l'Homme et du Citoyen* that was published in the Revolution's early days. Lafayette invited Paine over to Paris to see for himself, and thus it was the most uplifting early moments of the struggle to which he was a witness: the time when the young Wordsworth could write 'Bliss was it in that dawn to be alive.' The bliss was not unalloyed. While Part One of *Rights of Man* was arousing radical sympathy in London, Paine himself was almost lynched in the street for failing to wear a revolutionary cockade. But this misunderstanding did not discourage him on the main point, nor did it dim his general enthusiasm.

Thus, when Edmund Burke up-ended his vials in November 1790, and issued an all-out denunciation of the events in France, Paine felt that it was he who stood the best chance of refuting the arguments of the counter-revolution. Not that he was without rivals in this project: lengthy responses to Burkism were also written by William Godwin, Joseph Priestley and the pioneer feminist Mary Wollstone-craft. This was proof in itself of the emergence of a radical and Romantic faction in the hitherto stable and reactionary atmos-phere of Britain. Certainly the authorities feared as much. They may not have known that Paine, after publishing Part One in London, had helped to found a Republican Club in Paris with the Marquis de Condorcet, but they could still smell the spread of sedition in King George's domain.

When Paine published the first part of *Rights of Man* in 1791, it sold as many as 50,000 copies almost at once, and led to the setting up of 'corresponding societies' and other sorts of dis-cussion group among working people – inspired by the 'Committees of Correspondence' that had kept American rev-olutionaries in touch with one another, from colony to colony, in the germinal days of the Revolution. The British govern-ment had by then signed an agreement to recognize American independence, and could hardly construe pro-American feeling as subversive in and of itself, so its agents contented themselves with secretly commissioning a slanderous profile of Paine, written by a Scots bureaucrat named George Chalmers and published under the *nom de plume* of Francis Oldys. All the familar libels against Paine – faithless to women, addicted to liquor, thoroughly unsound character – were recycled.

Many of the Paineites, including Paine himself, had been convinced – unfairly in my view – that Burke also had been paid to write his *Reflections*. But in fact Burke himself was not yet considered as all that 'sound' in Tory circles. His work for America and his savage exposure of colonialist theft in India had not endeared him to the establishment. Moreover, it had recently been found necessary to declare George III temporarily insane, and to set up a regency, so there was no especially urgent need on the part of the court or the Tories to call attention to a witty volume that ridiculed hereditary monarchy.

The publishing history of the book is of interest none the less, as showing how fragile the right to dissent actually was in those years. Having completed Part One on his fifty-fourth birthday, 29 January 1791, Paine made haste to take the manuscript to a printer named Joseph Johnson. The proposed publication deadline, of 22 February, was intended to coincide with the opening of Parliament and the birthday of George Washington. Mr Johnson was a man of some nerve and principle, as he had demonstrated by printing several radical replies to Burke (including the one by Mary Wollstonecraft) but he took fright after several heavy-footed visits from William Pitt's political police. On the day of publication, he announced that *Rights of Man* would not appear under the imprint of his press. Paine was obliged to dash down to Fleet Street, find a publisher with more fortitude, J. S. Jordan, and bring the unbound sheets to him on a cart. He then made a further dash to Paris to arrange for a French translation, and left the final arrangements with Jordan to be made by a group of friends including William Godwin, the author of *Political Justice*. A few copies of the original Johnson edition were bound but almost none of them survive: Professor John Keane has found one in a collection of pamphlets in the British Museum. On 13 March 1791, the Jordan edition was published at a cover price of three shillings.

However, when Paine dedicated the second volume of *Rights of Man* to Lafayette, and called for the spreading of the French Revolution across mainland Europe, the gloves started to come off. Prime Minister William Pitt, on 21 May 1792, issued on behalf of the Crown a 'Royal Proclamation' aimed at 'wicked and seditious writings'. On the same day Paine received a summons to appear in court and answer a charge of seditious libel. Further scurrilous pamphlets against Paine were issued, and paid for through a 'secret service fund'. From the pulpit, and often with the assistance of the bench, menacing rallies were inspired at which either Paine's work or Paine's effigy were publicly incinerated. Teachers, bookstore owners, small printers and local advocates of free expression found themselves subject to fines, closure and imprisonment. Behind these pseudo-legal proceedings stood a stage-army of tipsy thugs, paid for by local Tory worthies, and glad enough of the chance to rough up some dissenter or break his windows or – even more menacing to throne, altar and order, as in the case of Priestley – his profane scientific instruments.

But *Rights of Man* continued to circulate in spite of such ugly pogroms, and Paine continued to go about his business even when shadowed everywhere by police spies and informers, and followed home every night to the home of his good friend Thomas 'Clio' Rickman. The huge attention lavished upon him by a rattled ruling class may have slightly gone to his head. He exhibited some symptoms of hubris. In replying to the writ of seditious libel, he publicly insulted the Home Secretary, Henry Dundas, and made a crude pun at the expense of the raving George III, referring to him as 'His *Mad*-jesty'. Perhaps surprisingly, Dundas responded by postponing the date set for the hearing. But it may be that the plan of Pitt's government, all along, had not been to martyr Paine but to scare him into fleeing the country.

If this was in fact the case, then it counts as some kind of historical irony that the poet William Blake may have acted as Pitt's unknowing accomplice. In early September 1792, Paine was the speaker at a meeting of the 'Friends of Liberty', where he made a rousing address and spoke defiance to repression along with support for the principles of 1789. The following night, so the legend goes, he was on similarly good form at a gathering at a friend's house, when Blake came up to him and said: 'You must not go home, or you are a dead man.'

Whether this really happened or not, Paine must have been impressed by something or someone, because he started almost at once for Dover. He went in company with John Frost, a lawyer for the London Corresponding Society, and with Achille Audibert, who was an official of the French town of Calais. This town, among others, had voted to offer French citizenship to Paine and a number of other foreigners, and it is possible that Pitt's agents knew of it. (It would have been very ingenious of them to have planted the rumour of Paine's arrest or assassination with the author of 'Jerusalem' and *Songs of Innocence and Experience*, but perhaps they did.) At any rate, Paine was only briefly detained and searched at Dover, and then allowed to board the vessel for France. Always assuming that he took a last glance over his shoulder at the receding white cliffs, we can end this episode with two sentimental reflections.

First: that would have been the last glimpse Thomas Paine of Thetford ever had of the country of his birth. Second: the show trial that the British government put on, *in absentia*, three months later, showed that the spirit of English liberty had not quite been extinguished. At the Guildhall in December 1792, Spencer Perceval opened for the prosecution in the matter of Thomas Paine's seditious libel. (Perceval was later to become the first and only prime minister to be assassinated.) He specified the nature of the seditious libel, which was not just upon the monarch but upon the entire foundation laid by the 'Glorious Revolution' of 1688. In reply there rose Thomas Erskine, the Attorney General for the Prince of

Wales, yet a distinguished liberal. In a four-hour speech he asserted that the liberty of the press and of expression was beyond the power of any government or parliament to circumscribe: it was a natural and inborn right. He did not forget to add that repression of this right could lead to rebellion and disorder, but the force of his pragmatic arguments was much exceeded by the brilliance of his liberal ones. He also added an empirical point, which testified to the essential unity of Paine's work. Most of what was said against monarchy in *Rights of Man*, Erskine reminded his audience, had long been available in any bookshop under the celebrated title *Common Sense*, written by the very same author. The jury had been carefully packed by the state, and did not even wait to hear the prosecution's rebuttal before voting to convict, but far more memorable was the vast crowd which waited on the Guildhall steps, cheered Erskine as he left the court, and drew his carriage home by hand all the way to Serjeant's Inn. The cry of 'Paine and the Liberty of the Press' and 'Erskine and the Rights of Juries', was heard from an assembly as large as had ever called for 'Wilkes and Liberty'. These Englishmen would have to wait for more than a generation for political rights, but at least their radical tradition had been kept stoutly alive in the lean years.

In Calais, meanwhile, Paine was hoping to give history, and the cause of political rights, an energetic shove in the right direction. His reception at Calais could not have been more different from his enforced departure from England. At that period, the Revolution was still led by the faction known as the Gironde, which had invited several non-French figures to take French nationality. (The list included William Wilberforce and Joseph Priestley.) More than that, several *départements* of the newly elected French assembly had chosen such men to be their deputies. Of the four which had esteemed him in this manner, Paine chose the *Pas de Calais*. He was therefore welcomed as something more than an honorary citizen. After taking lodging at an inn on *La rue de l'égalité*, Paine was taken to a rapturous ceremony at the town hall, where he was confirmed as the town's deputy to the National Convention. By the end of September he was in Paris and delivering, to the American ambassador Gouverneur Morris, the letters from Charles Pinckney, the American ambassador to London, that he had managed to get past the British agents at Dover.

His time as French revolutionary parliamentarian was not a period of felicity. For one thing, his French was rudimentary and he had to be attended at all times by an interpreter. More distressing was the dawning realization that this was not to be, on French soil, a reenactment of the Philadelphia principles of 1776 and 1786. It was easy enough for the Republican Paine to support the early motion 'That royalty be abolished in France', but subsequent debates made it plain that a federal system was not to be the replacement. Rather, it was grandly announced that 'The French Republic is one and indivisible'. What this rhetoric concealed was centralization of power, allied with appeals to populism.

This difference became very plain in the course of two subsequent debates, on the nature of the law and the fate of the king. In the first debate, the leading Jacobin Georges-Jacques Danton proposed scrapping the existing judiciary and replacing it with a system of, in effect, 'people's courts'. French justice had long been a pliant tool of the Church and the monarchy, but this did not inhibit Paine from taking the floor, flanked by his friend Etienne Goupilleau as interpreter, and arguing strongly for an independent and professional judiciary. The speech was decidedly not a success, and Danton's resolution was easily passed. (It is from this period, incidentally, that we derive our most common as well as our most crude political metaphor. The Jacobin faction began to sit to the left of the president's chair in the assembly, and the Girondins to his right. By this rough measure, Paine could be said to have moved to the right by moving to France.)

Attempting to regain his position, Paine tried to repeat the effect of *Common Sense* and *The Crisis* by publishing *Lettre de Thomas Paine au Peuple Français* on 25 September 1792. Reminding his audience that 'liberty cannot be purchased by a wish', and mingling this admonition with attacks on the armies of European reaction that were then pressing against Paris, he concluded with an injunction to 'punish by instruction, not revenge'. He misjudged, or perhaps misunderstood, the Jacobin character. To the faction of Robespierre, Marat and Danton, these words sounded lame and feeble. They needed blood to water their liberty tree, and were not too choosy about whose blood that would be.

For a brief interlude, Paine served on a committee to draft a new French constitution. His chief ally was the celebrated liberal thinker (and rebutter of Malthus), the Marquis de Condorcet. Again, both men miscalculated. The eventual document was too long, too cumbersome and too reasonable. And in any case, the tides of war and revolution were running too strongly. In November 1792, the Convention met to decide on the fate of the deposed King Louis, now contemptuously referred to by his family name of Louis Capet. The 1791 Constitution, which declared his person 'sacred and inviolable', was still in force. But the Jacobins sought to override this Constitution by claiming that Louis had committed further treason by intriguing with foreign powers (as indeed he had). They moved swiftly to propose his immediate execution, and they strongly implied culpable weakness or worse on the part of those who had any reservations.

Paine had two very important reservations. He thought that the king should not be executed at all, and he thought that in any event he should have a trial. There were some political justifications to be advanced here: American opinion would be adversely affected by the killing of a man who had once been an ally of the embryo United States, and a public trial might help expose the connections between the French monarchists and various unsavoury European despots currently making war on France. But Paine did not confine himself to tactical reasoning. He feared that an improvised debate followed by an execution would be charting the wrong course for the Revolution. He accordingly wrote another pamphlet, entitled *On the Propriety of Bringing Louis XVI to Trial*. Dismissing the absurd idea that Louis's person was 'sacred and inviolable', he none the less argued that 'an avidity to punish is always dangerous to liberty' because it can accustom a nation 'to stretch, to misinterpret, and to misapply even the best of laws'. In an appeal that was partly to compassion and partly to reason, he offered the maxim that: 'He that would make his own liberty secure must guard even his own enemy from repression; for if he violates this duty he establishes a precedent that will reach to himself.'

This sentence, and its implications, have haunted every revolution and counter-revolution ever since. Oddly enough, they struck a chord in at least one Jacobin writer, who defended free speech on the grounds that if today censorship was inflicted on the voices of reaction, then 'tomorrow silence will be laid on the Thomas Paines, the J. J. Rousseaus; for a policy which begins by closing the mouths of servile and cowardly pamphleteers because they can do harm, will end by depriving of utterance the generous defenders of the rights of man'.

Robespierre's response to this attitude was, in its way, no less eloquent. 'Those who talk of fair trials and the rule of law are unprincipled. Down with the principles of the *ancien régime.*' As if the *ancien régime* had represented fair trials and the rule of law...

Louis was brought to the Convention in December 1792 and subjected to a three-hour interrogation under which, despite his refusal to answer or even to hear some of the most incriminating questions, he bore up with some dignity. The Jacobins moved for an immediate vote on his conviction and execution, but the matter was deferred to the following month and (therefore) year ('Year One' of the Revolution having been proclaimed in 1792, with a subsequent short-lived attempt to change the names of the calendar months).

The debate in the Convention between 15 and 17 January 1793 occasioned one of Paine's most lonely hours, and very nearly cost him his own life. Resorting again to his favourite weapon, the printing press, he composed yet another pamphlet: *Opinion de Thomas Paine sur l'affaire de Louis Capet*. It was read to the delegates and evidently had a powerful effect on them, for they only decided by a majority of one to recommend the death of their former absolute ruler. Paine's argument was a classically liberal one. Public torture and execution was the problem, not the answer. It was the very signature of what France was trying to transcend, or to leave behind: 'It becomes us to be strictly on our guard against the abomination and perversity of monarchical examples: as France has been the first of European nations to abolish royalty, let her also be the first to abolish the punishment of death.'

These were the Enlightenment days in which the celebrated work of Cesare Beccaria, *On Crimes and Punishments*, had influenced numerous European and American figures to repudiate medieval methods of terrifying deterrence and retribution. But such thoughts were alien to the Jacobins, who wished to show by a stroke of the blade that there was no going back. They also brushed away Paine's suggestion that the king be rehabilitated by exile in America. Nor had they any time for his historic example of the banishment of the Stuart dynasty, which had withered after its exile from England. A roll-call of votes was announced, and more than a day was devoted to the spectacle of member after member announcing his vote and his reasons. The two non-French delegates took opposite sides of the question. Anacharsis Cloots, the colourful revolutionary aristocrat from Holland, denounced Louis for high treason and demanded his death 'in the name of the human race'. Paine, speaking in French for the first time, voted 'for the confinement of Louis until the end of the war, and for his perpetual banishment after the war'. When the votes were tallied, 287 had voted with Paine, 77 for death with a recommendation of clemency and 361 for death without conditions or delays.

Perhaps irritated by this less than imposing majority, and by Paine's later address reminding France of its dependence on the friendship of America, no less a revolutionary hero than the charismatic Jean-Paul Marat interjected that Paine had no right to a vote on the matter. 'He is a Quaker, and of course his religious views run counter to the infliction of capital punishment.' This sectarian innuendo did not prevent Paine from appealing one last time: 'Do not, I beseech you, bestow upon the English tyrant the satisfaction of learning that the man who helped America, the land of my love, to burst her fetters has died upon the scaffold.' Marat thereupon repeated his inaccurate anti-Quaker slur. The Convention voted again and confirmed the verdict, which two days later, on 21 January, was carried out.

The law which states that revolutions devour their own children is apparently an inexorable one. Within a few months, following battlefield reverses that had shaken the nerve of the leadership, the same Convention was facing furious demands that it be bled and purged. This hysteria against the enemy within was also led by Marat, who inaugurated a campaign to unmask all traitors. Among the many who were sent to the guillotine as a result was Anacharsis Cloots. Indeed, it became as dangerous to be a foreigner in this diseased atmosphere as it was to be a suspected faintheart. Paine was in double jeopardy. As he wrote to Thomas Jefferson in April 1793: 'Had this Revolution been conducted consistently with its principles, there was once a good prospect of extending liberty through the greatest part of Europe; but I now relinquish that hope.'

The remainder of this chapter can be fairly shortly told. After repeated confrontations with Marat, one of them in court and one of them by means of a letter from Paine that has been lost to history, the author of *Rights of Man* was arrested one night at Christmas 1793, just as he was completing work on *The Age of Reason*. The Robespierre 'Terror' had begun in earnest. As one of the Revolution's earliest enthusiasts, William Wordsworth, put it: 'Domestic carnage now filled the whole year. Friends, enemies, of all parties, ages, ranks, head after head, and never enough heads for those that bade them fall.'

It could be that Paine was lucky to be one of the first to experience confinement in the Luxembourg prison, because he avoided the 'domestic carnage' that stalked outside the walls. And at least some of his American friends knew where he was, and could try to intercede for him (though the ambassador, Gouverneur Morris, disgraced himself forever by failing to exert any serious pressure). However, conditions inside the prison became consistently worse as the demand for heads increased, and it could only have been a matter of time before Paine was listed for next day's butcher-bill. When that time did come, he was saved by a macabre accident. The chalk mark on the door of his cell, scheduling him for execution, was made by a stupid warder while the door was still open. When it was swung shut again, the number was on the wrong side. This secular version of a 'Passover' took place on 24 July 1794. Four days later the wheel of revolution revolved once more, and Maximilien Robespierre was himself sent to the guillotine. With the immediate threat of death removed, and with the arrival in Paris of a new and more sympathetic ambassador – the future president James Monroe – Paine's release was assured after a few more gruelling months.

His remaining years in France give the impression of the sour aftermath of a love affair. He was not trusted to leave the country as he had wished, and to return to America, but he was offered handsome apologies and the return of his seat in the Convention (with back-pay for the time spent sweltering in the Luxembourg). In a debate on the new Constitution of 1795, he once again took up his pen to criticize – unsuccessfully – the abolition of universal male suffrage. But the Convention itself was going into eclipse, and efforts to prolong its own life led to a riot in Paris on 5 October of that year. This was put down in the most unsentimental fashion by a Corsican officer of the name of Napoleon Bonaparte, who did not hesitate to employ cannon and shot against the crowd. The grave-digger of the Revolution had made his first appearance on the scene. On 4 September 1797, the irruption of the army into politics in its own right was confirmed by a military coup. All power was concentrated in the grip of a five-man 'Directory', held in place by bayonets and cannons.

Admirers of Paine must confront the unpleasant fact that he welcomed this seizure of power by an armed elite. He justified it, in speeches and on paper, as a necessary pre-emptive strike against a monarchist revival financed from London. It was true that Britain was backing restorationist forces with arms and money, but it was also true that Paine's loathing for King George and his prime minister had blinded him to reality both in France and England. He spent a great deal of his time playing the amateur general and strategist – not the musket-bearing footsoldier of yore – and evolving grandiose plans for the invasion and conquest of the British Isles. In Paris he met the great Irish Protestant republican Theobald Wolfe Tone and the dynamic Irish general James Napper Tandy, and applauded the French plan to land an army on Irish soil and surprise the British where they least expected it. (The pitiful failure of this scheme, which was actually attempted in 1798, is beautifully depicted in Thomas Flanagan's novel *The Year of the French*.)

Napoleon Bonaparte was at this stage, after his triumphs

in Austria and Italy, appointed the commander of a notional 'Army of England', which would – following the necessary annihilation of the British Navy – swarm across the Channel and ignite the flame of liberty among the oppressed subjects of the Hanoverian despotism. In this new capacity, he asked Paine to dinner. We only have one eye-witness to this extraordinary evening, on which the future Emperor swamped Paine with flattery, declared that he always slept with a copy of *Les Droits de l'Homme* under his pillow, and announced that a golden statue of its author should be erected 'in every city in the universe'. Possibly it was this confrontation with the Corsican in person that began to sow doubt in Paine: at any rate he is supposed to have become very much more modest about his knowledge of English conditions, to have later warned Bonaparte that the English would fight hard, and to have recommended a combination of economic and diplomatic warfare. This sudden softness disgusted the impatient *generalissimo*.

Whether Paine knew it or not, from his now rather tenuous connections with England, the term 'English' was metamorphosing into the neologism of 'British'. The long war against France had helped shape a wider national identity (excellently captured by Professor Linda Colley in her book *Britons: Forging the Nation, 1707–1837*) and was also forcing even political radicals to reconsider their patriotism. To recur to Patrick O'Brian's novel sequence, there were aboard King George's ships many men who had considerable sympathy for the ideals of the Cromwellian, American and French

Revolutions. However, the sheer exorbitance of Bonapartism
– Napoleon had himself crowned Emperor by Pope Pius in
1801, and signed a Concordat with the Vatican restoring
Catholicism as the official religion of France – was to make
them fairly cheerful fighters against French imperialism, and
to provide the British with a new species of Protestant folk-
hero. John Clare, the great melancholy poet of the English
countryside and its human and animal inhabitants, all made
void and defenceless by the 'enclosure' movement and its
annexation of what had once been common land, was later to
use a definitive metaphor, in his elegiac poem 'Remem-
brances', in trying to describe the sense of desecration and
loss:

By Langley bush I roam but the bush hath left its hill
On cowper green I stray, 'tis a desert strange and chill
And spreading lea close oak ere decay had penned its will
To the axe of the spoiler and self-interest fell a prey.
And cross berry way and old round oaks narrow lane
With its hollow trees like pulpits I shall never see again
Inclosure like a Buonaparte let not a thing remain
It levelled every bush and tree and levelled every hill
And hung the moles for traitors – though the brook is
    running still
It runs a naked brook cold and chill.

To instance Bonaparte as the ruthless prototype of the
landlord and the gamekeeper was, to say the least, to have

repudiated the idea of a foreign monarch as the friend of the English common folk. Men like William Hazlitt and Percy Bysshe Shelley may have maintained a sneaking sympathy for Bonaparte but not even in the years of black reaction after the 1815 Congress of Vienna – the years of Castlereagh and Metternich – was there to be any serious nostalgia for him except among certain operatic elements in France.

Those who had retained illusions about the French Revolution even in its newly militarized form were to be chilled permanently by the events of 9 November 1799. Known to some later historians as the 'Eighteenth Brumaire', after the Robespierrean calendar date on which it occurred, it was the day on which Napoleon arrogated all power to himself, proclaimed himself France's 'First Consul', and announced that the Revolution was at an end. This consummation of the earlier *coup d'état* appears to have broken the main spring for Paine. According to the same witness who gives us the account of that earlier 'statues of gold' dinner party; an Englishman with the almost roast-beef name of Henry Redhead Yorke, Paine was to describe Napoleon as 'the completest charlatan that ever existed'. The English poet Walter Savage Landor, who called upon Paine a little later in 1802, found him expressing the view that the First Consul was 'Wilful, headstrong, proud, morose, presumptuous... There is not on record one who has committed so many faults and crimes with so little temptation to commit them... Tyrants in general shed blood upon plan or from passion: he seems to have shed it only because he could not be quiet'.[2]

Paine did not put anything like this in print – his friend Nicholas Bonneville had been much persecuted for publishing criticisms of the new regime in his own paper *Le Bien Informé* – but he must have recognized that the atmosphere was thickening unpleasantly, as it had during the Robespierre terror. More than once, he attracted the attention of the Paris police, whose chauvinistic suspicion of foreigners had not abated. Hearing from his old friend Thomas Jefferson, now president, that a welcome back to America was offered to him, he essentially gave up France as a bad job and on the first day of September 1802 managed to book himself passage on a ship from the port of Le Havre that was bound for Baltimore.

In the United States, he had sought to make the revolution more radical, especially with respect to slavery and freethinking and the extension of democracy, and had been on the 'Left' side of the debate. In France, he had sought to make the revolution more temperate and humane, taking his place to the 'Right' of the chair. Now he had fallen victim to a gigantic counter-revolution in revolutionary disguise, which had succeeded in entrenching rather than undermining his original foes: the British monarchy and British Toryism. Thomas Paine was one of the first to experience the full effect of modern absolutist ideology in all of its early forms: his life could be seen as a prefiguration of what would happen to idealists and revolutionaries in the following century.

CHAPTER 3

Rights of Man, Part One

The foregoing is a necessary prelude to an understanding of the never-ending debate between Edmund Burke and Thomas Paine. This classic exchange between two masters of polemic is rightly considered to be the ancestor of all modern arguments between Tories and radicals, or between those who believe in tradition and property and heredity and those who distrust or abhor them. But, just as the left/right division in the French Convention proved to be simplistic and misleading, so it can be a mistake to caricature either antagonist in this combat. As I mentioned earlier, Burke was not an English Tory. He was an Irish Whig, with an attachment to Catholicism which he may have had good reason – under the penal laws enacted in the Ireland of his birth – to keep quiet about. He was attacked in his own day, by both Thomas Jefferson and Thomas Paine, for accepting a small pension from the British government for services rendered. This modest payment was, for them, proof positive that Burke had 'sold out' and abandoned his liberal principles. The point is worth stressing, if only because it reminds us that in the view of his contemporaries at least, Burke had had some principles in the first place. His open letter to the electors of his Bristol constituency is still the essential defence of the duty of a parliamentary representative to follow his conscience rather than be a mere delegate or an envoy. His support for the American colonists, his sympathy for Ireland, and his long campaign for justice for the Indian subjects of British rule were evidence of that. Jefferson implicitly conceded as much when he wrote to his friend Benjamin Vaughan in May 1791:

> The Revolution of France does not astonish me so much as
> the revolution of Mr Burke. I wish I could believe the latter
> proceeded from as pure motives as the former... How morti-
> fying that this evidence of the rottenness of his mind must
> oblige us now to ascribe to wicked motives those actions of
> his life which wore the mark of virtue and patriotism.[1]

Jefferson's final appeal to George III on behalf of the colonists – *A Summary View of the Rights of British America* – had been reviewed and edited by Burke before it went to the press. It was the last argument with official obduracy before the Declaration of Independence. At the time, Burke had also been a parliamentary lobbyist for the colony of New York, and had received payment for that service as well. In a foot-note to volume I of *Das Kapital*, Karl Marx was later forced to admit in all honesty that if Burke had been a mercenary against the French Revolution, he had also been a mercenary in favour of the American one. As he put it:

The sycophant – who in the pay of the English oligarchy
played the romantic *laudator temporis acti* against the French
revolution just as, in the pay of the North American colonies
at the beginning of the American troubles, he had played the
liberal against the English oligarchy – was an out-and-out
vulgar bourgeois.[2]

It is a deformity in some 'radicals' to imagine that, once
they have found the lowest or meanest motive for an action or
for a person, they have correctly identified the authentic or
'real' one. Many a purge or show trial has got merrily under
way in this manner.

Burke was a much more formidable opponent than that.
One ought to begin with a sense of what animated his
extreme alarm at the very first news of the events of July
1789. If we consult the title-page of his original 1790
Reflections on the Revolution in France, we will find that it is
actually called 'Reflections on the Revolution in France,
and on the Proceedings in Certain Societies in London
Relative to That Event: In a Letter Intended to Have Been
Sent to a Gentleman in Paris'. The 'gentleman' in question
was Charles-Jean-François Depont, a young Frenchman of
Burke's acquaintance who had become a member of the
French National Assembly in 1789 and who had written to
him in the autumn of 1789. The 'Reflections' were Burke's
long apology for a delayed response. 'The Revolution in
France', rather than the plainer 'French Revolution', seems
to have expressed Burke's belief that 'revolution' was on

the march, and France only one of its actual or potential theatres.

He had been further stirred to put pen to paper by a report of two gatherings in London, of the Revolution Society and the Society for Constitutional Information, both of which had passed warm resolutions welcoming the fall of the Bastille. The 'Constitutional' Society was more radical than its name implied, and the Revolution Society less so, but it was the preamble to the Revolution Society's resolution that appalled Burke. It read: 'This Society, sensible of the important advantages arising to this Country by its deliverance from Popery and arbitrary power...'

Now, ostensibly, the Revolution Society was a respectable club, dedicated to the celebration of the so-called 'Glorious Revolution' of 1688, that relatively bloodless coup that had installed William and Mary of the House of Orange on the throne of England, and established Protestantism as the official state religion. And, ostensibly, one of the Society's leaders, the Reverend Richard Price, was a solid Unitarian clergyman who had, like Burke, been a keen advocate of American rights. But to Burke this sentence was a trumpet of alarm. Ten years previously, in 1780, the authorities had completely lost control of London in days and nights of vicious rioting and looting, known to history as 'the Gordon riots'. Lord George Gordon, a rather demented aristocratic demagogue, had raised the mob against a supposed secret Catholic conspiracy, which would rivet the fetters of Rome on honest English folk. (The best evocation of the poisonous atmosphere of the time, and of its bloody outcome, is to be found in Dickens's *Barnaby Rudge*.) This memory was very much alive in Edmund Burke's mind, and goes far to explain his loathing for mass populism. In the vast crowds mobilized by Gordon, there had been a large contingent carrying American flags and yelling pro-American slogans. Not even the good Reverend Price had been immune to Gordon's seductions. In Burke's mind, there was a clear and threatening connection between the anti-clericalism of the Jacobins across the Channel and the anti-Catholicism of their English sympathizers.

This slight element of paranoia, with its accompanying shudder of distaste for the unwashed masses, disfigured Burke's book in some important ways. He himself was not quite grand enough to make his snobbery and condescension either convincing or forgivable. Nor was he always able to bring off a good sneer. In *Common Sense*, Thomas Paine had made the reasonable witticism that 'Government, like dress, is the badge of lost innocence'. Burke's scorn for those who thought 'that government may vary like modes of dress' was a clumsily point-missing riposte. Other shafts at the friends of democracy and universal suffrage made up with venom what they lacked in relevance:

> The occupation of an hair-dresser, or of a working tallow-chandler, cannot be a matter of honour to any person – to say nothing of other more servile employments. Such descriptions of men ought not to suffer oppression from the state;

but the state suffers oppression, if such as they, either
individually or collectively, are permitted to rule.[3]

To this, for good measure, he added some verses from
Ecclesiastes: 'How can he get wisdom that holdeth the plough,
and that glorieth in the goad; that driveth oxen; and is
occupied in their labours; and whose talk is of bullocks?' This
was a long way from those other 'reflections', of Thomas
Gray in a country churchyard as dusk came on. After all, the
most that the Reverend Price had apparently asserted was
that, by means of the 1688 Revolution, the people had
acquired three basic rights: '(1) To choose our own governors
(2) To cashier them for misconduct (3) To frame a government for ourselves'. Burke set himself to prove that no such
rights existed, and that English people were bound by a kind
of organic contract of eternal allegiance.

In other passages of the *Reflections*, Burke veered bizarrely
from the crudely authoritarian to the moistly sentimental. He
bluntly described the sympathizers of revolution as guilty of
'sedition' – which was then a seriously punishable crime –
and called for them to be silenced by the authorities. In some
fashion that none of his biographers has quite managed to
analyze, he identified proper authority with the male principle, and asserted 'masculine morality' as against (one of his
most celebrated phrases) 'the swinish multitude'. Yet his
most celebrated flight of rhetoric was a paean to the entirely
arbitrary power and charm of a woman who was not even
French – the idle and capricious Austrian Marie Antoinette.

There is no alternative to the quotation of this passage in full:

It is now sixteen or seventeen years since I saw the Queen of France, then the Dauphiness, at Versailles; and surely never lighted on this orb, which she hardly seemed to touch, a more delightful vision. I saw her just above the horizon, decorating and cheering the elevated sphere she just began to move in, – glittering like the morning-star, full of life, and splendour, and joy. Oh! What a revolution! And what an heart must I have to contemplate without emotion that elevation and that fall! Little did I dream when she added titles of veneration to those of enthusiastic, distant, respectful love, that she should ever be obliged to carry the sharp antidote to disgrace concealed in that bosom; little did I dream that I should have lived to see such disasters fallen upon her in a nation of gallant men, in a nation of men of honour, and of cavaliers. I thought ten thousand swords must have leaped from their scabbards to avenge even a look that threatened her with insult. – But the age of chivalry is gone. – That of sophisters, economists and calculators, has succeeded; and the glory of Europe is extinguished for ever. Never, never more shall we behold that generous loyalty to rank and sex, that proud submission, that dignified obedience, that subordination of the heart, which kept alive, even in servitude itself, the spirit of an exalted freedom. The unbought grace of life, the cheap defence of nations, the nurse of manly sentiment and heroic enterprise, is gone! It is gone, that sensibility of principle, that chastity of honour, which felt a stain like a wound, which inspired courage whilst it mitigated ferocity, which ennobled whatever it touched, and under which vice itself lost half its evil, by losing all its grossness.[4]

One takes a deep inhalation at the end of this, and marvels that it is the Romantics who are supposed to have *supported* the French Revolution! Surely no more floridly romantic paragraph of pseudo-chivalry was ever composed, either in earnest or in jest, since the quill of Miguel de Cervantes was replaced in its scabbard? Perhaps slightly sensitive on this very point, Burke swelled himself with quixotic indignation at an early stage in the *Reflections* to demand of his unseen audience:

Am I to congratulate an highwayman and murderer, who has broke prison, upon the recovery of his natural rights? This would be to act over again the scene of the criminals condemned to the galleys, and their heroic deliverer, the metaphysic Knight of the Sorrowful Countenance.[5]

I shall delay giving Paine's response to this: Burke was temporarily more annoyed by the reaction of his friend Philip Francis, to whom he had sent the draft and the proofs of his essay. The amity between the two men cooled rapidly when Francis responded:

In my opinion all that you say of the Queen is pure
foppery. If she be a perfect female character you ought to
take your ground upon her virtues. If she be the reverse it
is ridiculous in any but a Lover, to place her personal
charms in opposition to her crimes. Either way I know the
argument must proceed upon a supposition; for neither
have you said anything to establish her moral merits, nor
have her accusers formally tried and convicted her of guilt.[6]

Francis, who wrote scathing pamphlets under the pseudonym of 'Junius' and who had been a close comrade of Burke's
during the Warren Hastings affair, ended by urging him to
abandon the whole project. He was made especially uneasy
by Burke's partisanship for 'The Church' which, he added,
was the very same 'religion, in short, which was practiced or
professed, and with very great Zeal too, by tyrants and vil-
lains of every denomination'. This caught Burke on the raw.
He was above all concerned to uphold the authority of the
Church against atheism, and against those 'deists' who he
believed provided the smokescreen for godlessness. So
furious was he on this point that he did not even try to discuss
the work of the French *philosophes*. Their secular and rationalist critique did not deserve to be mentioned. As he phrased it
in a footnote to the *Reflections*: 'I do not choose to shock the
feeling of the moral reader with any quotation of their vulgar,
base, and profane language.'[7] So much for the encyclopaed-
ists, dismissed but not debated. In 1797, the year of his death,
Burke wrote to the exiled Abbé Barruel to thank him in the

most fulsome tones for a copy of his *Mémoires pour server à l'histoire du Jacobinisme*. Barruel's work was infamous even in its time as a specimen of diseased Jesuitical paranoia, blaming all the ills of France and the world on a subversive Freemason conspiracy. In a later time, such propaganda was to be one of the elements of European fascism, but the fastidious and anti-mobbish Burke praised it for its justice, regularity and exactitude.

Conor Cruise O'Brien, Burke's most exhaustive and brilliant biographer and exegete, has speculated that Burke's strenuous attack on revolution in France was motivated partly by a desire to plead, if only by indirection, for reform in Ireland. By impressing the centre and the right of British politics, runs the argument, Burke could earn the right to argue that concessions should be made to his oppressed and Catholic fellow countrymen. This hypothesis seems completely convincing. Burke saw that any 'United Irishman' rebellion, of the sort favoured by Paine and others, would lead to a long period of British reaction and counterrevolution, especially if it could be argued that Irish rebellion was being fomented from Paris.

O'Brien, however, does not spend enough time considering the corollary. If Burke was really writing about Ireland in the *Reflections*, and encoding a 'message' to the political establishment of his day, then he was also writing about England. And, strangely enough for a covert Catholic, he was writing about the 'Glorious Revolution' of 1688 in almost exactly the same terms of approbation as those employed by that anti-papist, the Reverend Richard Price. Burke wrote of the events of 1688 and 1689, which included the Declaration of Rights, as if history had come to a full stop in those years, and had produced a perfect Constitution for Britain, made even more perfect if possible by the wonderful fact of its being unwritten: 'So far is it from being true, that we acquired a right by the Revolution to elect our kings, that if we had possessed it before, the English nation did at that time most solemnly renounce and abdicate it, for themselves and for all their posterity for ever.'

Rather cleverly, Burke took up the idea of which English radicals were most fond – the idea that the freedom of the people was inherited and transmitted from the past – and used it to reinforce the hereditary principle in general. 'No experience has taught us that in any course of method save that of an *hereditary crown*, our liberties can be regularly per-petuated and preserved sacred as our *hereditary right*.' Indeed, 'We have an inheritable crown; an inheritable peerage; and an house of commons and a people inheriting privileges, fran-chises, and liberties, from a long line of ancestors'.

Radicalism and anti-monarchism were thus condemned by definition, since the 'ancient fundamental principles' were already emplaced and embedded, and since 'the very idea of the fabrication of a new government is enough to fill us with disgust and horror'. Burke's intelligence is on full display here, since he is meeting his critics on their own ground and challenging them to assert heredity in one way, and to deny it in another, without contradicting themselves. The paradox, of course, is this: the 1688 Revolution actually deposed King James II and put an end to his hereditary lineage. Was this something that could only be done once, or that could furnish no precedent? Keep your eye, therefore, on that word 'fabricated'. With these and other fulminations, Burke seemed to be mutating from Whiggery through Toryism and into a full-blown reactionary.

Yet there were moments in the *Reflections* when he achieved near-mastery as a composer of political prose. The first instance I shall give is a statement of what might be termed 'human nature' conservatism, even if slightly dressed up in contempt for what the aristocracy would then have called 'trade', and which later critics were to describe as 'the cash nexus':

> The state ought not to be considered as nothing better than a partnership agreement in a trade of pepper and coffee, calico or tobacco, or some other such low concern… *It becomes a partnership not only between those who are living, but between those who are living, those who are dead, and those who are to be born.* Each contract of each particular state is but a clause in the great primaeval contract of eternal society, linking the lower with the higher natures, connecting the visible and invisible world, according to a fixed compact sanctioned by the inviolable oath which holds all physical and moral natures, each in their appointed place. [Italics are mine][8]

Pursuing this penetrating analysis, which might be

described as anti-capitalist *avant de la lettre*, Burke foresaw a rampantly corrupt France in which, with all customary bonds dissolved, the country would become

> wholly governed by the agitators in corporations, by
> societies in the towns formed of directors of *assignats* and
> trustees for the sale of church lands, attorneys, agents,
> money-jobbers, speculators, and adventurers, composing an
> ignoble oligarchy, founded on the destruction of the crown,
> the church, the nobility, and the people. Here end all the
> deceitful dreams and visions of the equality and rights
> of men.[9]

The man who Karl Marx later dismissed as 'an out-and-out vulgar bourgeois' had anticipated him by sketching the outlines of a bourgeois revolution.

It must at all times be borne in mind that Burke was writing when the French Revolution was in its first flush of youthful enthusiasm, and was provoking similar flushes in others. This is what makes his next paragraphs so utterly arresting. In 1790 he was able to write:

> It is known; that armies have hitherto yielded a very
> precarious and uncertain obedience to any senate, or
> popular authority; and they will least of all yield it to an
> assembly which is only to have a continuance of two years.
> The officers must totally lose the characteristic disposition
> of military men, if they see with perfect submission and

due admiration, the domination of pleaders; especially
when they find that they have a new court to pay to an
endless succession of those pleaders; whose military policy,
and the genius of whose command (if they should have
any) must be as uncertain as their duration is transient.[10]

This might have been written by anyone who had studied
military matters in a time of political flux. But most striking is
the continuation:

> In the weakness of one kind of authority, and in the
> fluctuation of all, the officers of an army will remain for
> some time mutinous and full of faction, *until some popular*
> *general, who understands the art of conciliating the soldiery, and*
> *who possesses the true spirit of command, shall draw the eyes of*
> *all men upon himself.* Armies will obey him on his personal
> account. There is no other way of securing military
> obedience in this state of things. But the moment in which
> that event shall happen, the person who really commands
> your army is your master; the master (that is little) of your
> king, the master of your Assembly, the master of your
> whole republic. [Italics mine].[11]

This is an almost supernaturally prescient account of the way
in which the French Revolution would develop in practice.
One is compelled to wonder whether Thomas Paine ever
recalled it, during the long and arduous and frustrating
decade in which he lived through the unfolding of Burke's

predictions. I do not know of any more chillingly accurate forecast, with the exception of Rosa Luxemburg's famous warning to Lenin, in 1918, that Bolshevik methods would lead, first, to the dictatorship of one party, and then to a dictatorship of that party's central committee, and finally to absolute rule by one member of that central committee. (Luxemburg's favourite pseudonym was 'Junius', for Lucius Junius Brutus – not the Shakespearean regicide Brutus but the hero and founder of the Roman republic. This makes it the more apt, if only in retrospect, that Burke's friend and critic Philip Francis employed the same pseudonym.)

Along with our use of the terms 'left' and 'right', we have another means of distinguishing our political and intellectual animals. It was taken by Isaiah Berlin from the ancient philosopher Archilocus, who observed that 'the fox knows many things, but the hedgehog knows one big thing'. The distinction is not hard and fast, any more than other sheep-and-goats separations are hard and fast (one thinks of the attempt to sort all English intellectuals into the categories of Roundhead and Cavalier, or Edmund Wilson's classifying of all Americans as either Redskins or Palefaces); and it occasionally happens that men are foxes and hedgehogs combined. Both Burke and Paine knew many things, and each knew one big thing as well. For Burke, the big thing was that the French Revolution would come to grief, and worse. For Paine, the big thing was that the age of chivalry was indeed dead, in that hereditary monarchy was doomed to give way to a democracy based on suffrage rather than property.

This is not to split the difference and to say that both men were right. The exchange between them was extremely bitter, and though the gap was sometimes narrow it was invariably deep. Just to give one illustration: Paine, as we have seen, took many more risks than Edmund Burke to save the life of the monarch Burke so much admired (and, by extension, the lives of his queen and his children). But he had no time to waste on a recitation of Marie Antoinette's imaginary charms, and dismissed Burke's panegyric in one curt line: 'He pities the plumage, but forgets the dying bird.' Nor did he fail to take Burke up on the matter of the Cervantes analogy. 'In the rapture of his imagination, he has discovered a world of windmills, and his sorrows are, that there are no Quixotes to attack them.'

Paine's main assault, however, was on Burke's unsafe assumption that the historic legitimacy of the 1688 monarchy was something that existed in an ethereal region that was beyond all critique. He seized particularly on Burke's repeated use of the words 'for ever' to describe the emplacement of the Glorious Revolution:

> There never did, there never will, and there never can exist a
> parliament, or any description of men, or any generation of
> men, in any country, possessed of the right or the power of
> binding and controlling posterity to the 'end of time,' or of
> commanding for ever how the world should be governed, or
> who shall govern it: and therefore, all such clauses, acts or
> declarations, by which the makers of them attempt to do

what they have neither the right nor the power to do, nor the power to execute, are in themselves null and void. Every age and generation must be as free to act for itself, *in all cases*, as the ages and generations which preceded it. The vanity and presumption of governing beyond the grave is the most ridiculous and insolent of all tyrannies.[12]

The effect of these words on newly literate artisans, who had seen others be imprisoned or transported merely for criticism of the British monarchy, can well be imagined. But Paine was not done with his repudiation of hereditary or entrenched power. In a line which could have been used in one of his essays against the slave trade, he proclaimed: 'Man has no property in man.' He continued:

Neither has any generation a property in the generations which are to follow. The parliament or the people of 1688, or of any other period, has no more right to dispose of the people of the present day, or to bind or to control them *in any shape whatever*, than the parliament or the people of the present day have to dispose of, bind or control those who are to live a hundred or a thousand years hence. Every generation is, and must be, competent to all the purposes which its occasions require. It is the living, and not the dead, that are to be accommodated. When man ceases to be, his power and his wants cease with him; and having no longer any participation in the concerns of this world, he has no longer any authority in directing who shall be its

governors, or how its government shall be organized, or
how administered.[13]

This belief, that 'the earth belongs to the living', had already
been the subject of a disagreement between Thomas Jefferson
and James Madison during the debate on the American constitution. Madison had reminded his old friend that previous
generations built bridges, planted trees and made investments
for posterity to enjoy, so that no very sharp distinction between
succeeding epochs should be drawn. Furthermore, it can be
dangerous to make the attempt: the French institution of a new
calendar and a new age was not only destined to wither within
one generation, but also to serve as a warning that a 'Year Zero'
is a bad beginning. But Paine, who took the Jeffersonian side
in this dispute, also took his chief example from Jefferson's
work. The English monarchy derived in reality not from the
supposed settlement of 1688, but from the Norman Conquest
of 1066. It was Paine's expressed hope that a foreign imposition
from one part of France would eventually be undone by the
revolutionary inspiration of the whole. 'Conquest and tyranny
transplanted themselves with William the Conqueror from
Normandy into England, and the country is yet disfigured
with the marks. May then the example of all France contribute
to regenerate the freedom which a province of it destroyed!'
Relishing this contrast, he proceeded to rub it in:

In the addresses of the English Parliaments to their Kings,
we see neither the intrepid spirit of the old Parliaments of

France, nor the serene dignity of the present National
Assembly; neither do we see in them anything of the style
of English manners, which borders somewhat on bluntness.
Since then they are neither of foreign extraction, nor
naturally of English production, their origin must be sought
for elsewhere, and that origin is the Norman Conquest.
They are evidently of the vassalage class of manners, and
emphatically mark the prostrate distance that exists in no
other condition of men than between the conqueror and the
conquered. That this vassalage idea and style of speaking
was not got rid of even at the Revolution of 1688, is evident
from the declaration of Parliament to William and Mary, in
these words: 'We do most humbly and faithfully submit
ourselves, our heirs and posterities, for ever.' Submission is
wholly a vassalage term, repugnant to the dignity of
Freedom, and an echo of the language used at the
Conquest.[14]

Taking inspiration perhaps from his own 'blunt' rhetoric,
Paine ventured a bold prediction:

As the estimation of all things is by comparison, the
Revolution of 1688, however from circumstances it may have
been exalted beyond its value, will find its level. It is already
on the wane, eclipsed by the enlarging orb of reason, and the
luminous revolutions of America and France. In less than
another century, it will go, as well as Mr Burke's labours, 'to
the family vault of all the Capulets.' Mankind will then

scarcely believe that a country calling itself free, would send
to Holland for a man, and clothe him with power on purpose
to put themselves in fear of him, and give him almost a
million sterling a year for leave to *submit* themselves and
their posterity, like bond-man and bond-women, for ever.[15]

There are some obvious hostages to fortune here, in the
optimistic references to the French National Assembly, that
scarcely need to be pointed out at this date. But it is too easy to
forget, in a time of supposedly consultative and ceremonial
monarchy, how long and how late the idea of 'the Norman
yoke' survived in English and indeed in American conscious-
ness. Thomas Jefferson grounded his claim of American
rights on the ancient liberties of the Anglo-Saxons, which had
not been nullified by a Norman subjugation and which had
transferred themselves across the Atlantic and out of monarchy's reach. There was a popular joke in my own very conservative Hampshire grandfather's day about a dispute between
an English peasant tenant and his hereditary landlord. 'Do
you realize?' enquires the exasperated squire, 'that my ancestors came over with King William?' 'Yes,' replies the tenant.
'We were ready for you.' Rudyard Kipling preserved the idea
in his 1911 poem 'Norman and Saxon' in which an expiring
Norman aristocrat of the year 1100 offers some deathbed
advice to his son and heir:

> 'The Saxon is not like us Normans. His manners
>   are not so polite.

But he never means anything serious till he talks
    about justice and right.
When he stands like an ox in the furrow – with his
    sullen set eyes on your own,
And grumbles, 'This isn't fair dealing,' my son,
    leave the Saxon alone.'

Part of Paine's purpose, indeed, in writing *Rights of Man* in the way that he did, was to reform or purify the language of political discourse. By the abysmal literary and rhetorical standards of our own day, his prose seems to be limpid and muscular and elevated at the same time. But in 1791 it appeared to many loftier critics to be barbarously uncouth. Paine was unapologetic about this. 'As it is my design to make those that can scarcely read understand, I shall therefore avoid every literary ornament and put it in language as plain as the alphabet.' Having helped expel the inheritors of William and Mary from North America, he hoped to repeat the demotic success of *Common Sense* and *The Crisis* in the heartland of monarchy itself. His examples were almost all drawn from works – the Bible, the Book of Common Prayer and the plays of William Shakespeare – that even the unlettered might be expected to know at least partly by heart. His breaking of a lance with the Catholic courtier Edmund Burke was to be a repeat performance of those Protestant martyrs and militants, from William Tyndale to John Bunyan, who had insisted on a plain English bible and denied the right of a sly priesthood to conduct its business only in the arcane tongue of Latin.

Profanity, indeed, was one of his weapons of demystification. Who, after all, was William the Norman but a man of illegitimate birth: 'the son of a prostitute, and the plunderer of the English nation'? (A. J. Ayer pointed out drily that, by levelling this insult at William's bastard lineage, Paine ought really to have been paying a compliment to the Conqueror's lack of a hereditary claim.) Paine spoke in the same tones as had the peasant rebels Wat Tyler and John Ball, demanding to know by what right mere men could set themselves up as rulers, thus abolishing the natural rights and equality of God's creation. 'When Adam delved and Eve span,' as the rebels had demanded to know in 1381, 'Who was *then* the gentleman?' Updating this ancient and subversive riddle, Paine challenged Burke like this:

> Mr Burke, with his usual outrage, abuses the *Declaration of the Rights of Man*, published by the National Assembly of France as the basis on which the constitution of France is built. This he calls 'paltry and blurred sheets of paper about the rights of man'. Does Mr Burke mean to deny that *man* has any rights? If he does, then he must mean that there are no such things as rights anywhere, and that he has none himself; for who is there in the world but man? But if Mr Burke means to admit that man has rights, the question will then be: What are those rights, and how came man by them originally?[16]

This is a question that has still not been fully answered. Either the concept of 'right' has meaning or it is a selfish and solipsistic claim made by needy humans, with no objective basis for its assertion. Radicals as different as Bentham and Marx have taken the latter view, while the American Declaration of Independence changed the world by claiming that all children of the creator – it specified 'men' but excluded no-one by name – possessed rights that were 'inalienable'. This brave idea may have had no basis in reality, but it was impossible for the reactionaries to argue that the whole concept of 'right' was void. Had they not affirmed the divine right of kings? The best and most ironic way to proceed was to take this claim and simultaneously invert and expand it. Paine was an expert at this tactic, and he knew his two Testaments very well:

> It is not among the least of the evils of the present existing government in all parts of Europe, that man, considered as man, is thrown back to a vast distance from his Maker, and the artificial chasm filled up by a succession of barriers, or sort of turnpike gates, through which he has to pass. I will quote Mr Burke's catalogue of barriers that he has set up between man and his Maker. Putting himself in the character of a herald, he says: 'We fear God – we look with *awe* to kings – with affection to parliaments – with duty to magistrates – with reverence to priests, and with respect to nobility.' Mr Burke has forgotten to put in 'chivalry'. He has also forgotten to put in Peter.[17]

This is an almost perfect encapsulation of the Protestant

ethos, with its ideal of an unmediated relationship between mankind and the creator, requiring no priesthood or incense or stained glass. (Not that Paine was ever sectarian: he willingly conceded that the anti-Catholic bigot Lord George Gordon was 'a madman'.)

Thus, to Paine, all hereditary titles and honours were a mere human superimposition on the natural equality, and natural rights, of mankind. 'I have always considered monarchy to be a silly, contemptible thing,' he wrote. 'I compare it to something kept behind a curtain, about which there is a great deal of bustle and fuss, and a wonderful air of seeming solemnity, but when, by any accident, the curtain happens to open, and the company see what it is, they burst into laughter.' (Frank Baum was one day to make himself immortal by recasting this insight for children and entitling it *The Wizard of Oz*.) Again, Paine had his bible to hand as he emphasized the point, and praised the French Revolution for abolishing such man-made fripperies:

> Titles are but nick-names, and every nick-name is a title. The thing is perfectly harmless in itself: but it marks a sort of foppery in the human character, which degrades it. It renders man into the diminutive of man in things which are great, and the counterfeit of woman in things which are little. It talks about its fine *blue ribbon* like a girl, and shows its new *garter* like a child. A certain writer of some antiquity says: 'When I was a child, I thought as a child; but when I became a man, I put away childish things.'[18]

Paine also affirmed, in tones that seem to us more obviously modern:

> The greatest characters the world have known, have rose
> on the democratic floor. Aristocracy has not been able
> to keep a proportionate pace with democracy. The
> artificial NOBLE shrinks into a dwarf before the NOBLE
> of nature.[19]

There is an echo, here, of Robert Burns's best loved poem, 'For a'that':

> The rank is but the guinea's stamp
> The man's the gold for a'that.

And, while on the subject of natural rights and natural laws, Paine did not forget to point out that monarchy and aristocracy have a tendency both to overbreed and to inbreed. The rules of primogeniture require that more than one son or heir be born, in case of the need for a 'spare', and the rules of dynasty require that marriages be kept within a smallish circle of candidates. This creates what might be termed a 'disposal' problem, because the surplus children are 'to be provided for by the public, but at a greater charge', while 'unnecessary offices and places in governments and courts are created at the expense of the public, to maintain them'. If Burke's tear-stained evocation of Marie Antoinette was not equalled until the hysterical tributes to Diana Spencer – also 'martyred' in Paris – then which European royal house since 1791 has not lamented, like our very own Windsors, the ghastly problem of what to do with the proliferating, subsidized and under-achieving offspring?

Paine also emphasized that, so far from bringing the blessings of stability to England, its monarchs had embroiled the country in countless wars, foreign and domestic, simply in order to decide which sprig or twig of the ruling branch was to be the master. To Burke's proposed hereditary triad of crown, peers and commons, all three sustained by inherited rights, he opposed a triad of his own. The regimes that emerge out of human society 'may all be comprehended under three heads. First, Superstition. Secondly, Power. Thirdly, the common interest of society, and the common rights of man. The first was a government of priestcraft, the second of conquerors, and the third of reason.'[20]

Furthering this rather simplistic assertion, he denied that any pre-existing 'contract' between ruler and ruled could exist in any case. To believe that it had, as John Locke had and Edmund Burke did, was

putting the effect before the cause; for as man must have existed before governments existed, there necessarily was a time when governments did not exist, and consequently there could originally exist no governors to form such a compact with. The fact therefore must be, that the *individuals themselves*, each in his own personal and sovereign right, *entered into a compact with each other* to produce a govern-

ment: and this is the only mode in which governments have
a right to arise, and the only principle on which they have a
right to exist.[21]

He went on to write that 'governments must have arisen,
either *out* of the people, or *over* the people'.

This risks making a distinction without a difference, and
the risk is increased by Paine's interchangeable use of the
terms 'man' and 'individuals'. Society and government may
be quite distinct concepts but the study of history makes it
very difficult to determine that there ever was a society
without a government, let alone vice versa. There may have
been a pre-existing 'state of nature' but it does not seem to
have been enviable and most philosophers and anthropolo-
gists date the study of human culture from the indeterminate
moment when that very state was transcended, and succeeded by bonds of society, exchange, trade and so forth. At
that moment, it seems beside the point to argue whether early
societies submitted to an imposed leadership, or chose a
leader from among themselves, or permitted one to emerge. It
is absolutely certain that no deity had anything to do with the
process, just as it is certain that merely human authorities
have always sought to cloak themselves in supernatural or
superhuman claims, but that is as far as Paine ought to have
pushed the argument.

In his day, there was still an echo to the words of Rousseau,
a man much esteemed by Paine and much despised by Burke,
to the effect that, in his famous opening words to *The Social*

Contract, man was 'born free, but is everywhere in chains'. The first part of that claim might be held to be somehow objectively true, even of a child who thanks to the state of nature would be condemned to live in agony and starvation for a few days before expiring, but the suggestion that the chains only came later is a suggestion that makes the state of nature seem more attractive than any human has ever found it to be. It might be truer to say that the freedom and the chains are contemporaneous, since all children are born into a losing struggle with death and disappointment. Just as Paine's joke about dress and lost innocence was intended to remind his audience of a mythical Eden, so his appeal to a lost but golden and innocent past was a trope that Milton and Blake knew very well. There are two notorious problems with this concept of a lost Paradise, or lost innocence. The first is that nobody has ever been able to describe it in a manner that makes it seem remotely attractive (which is part of the reason for Blake's observation about *Paradise Lost*: that it showed Milton being 'of the devil's party without knowing it'). The second is that it is often used to imply an apocalyptic or millennial future: the sudden return or restoration of that lost or stolen ideal state. Rational and commonsensical as Paine was in his everyday applications, he was no more immune to these twin rhetorical temptations than any other revolutionary of his day, and he must bear some of the responsibility for the 'heaven on earth' propaganda, whether it referred to a mythical past or an unattainable future, that disordered the radical tradition thereafter.

The rest of Paine's reply to Burke, at least in Part One of

Rights of Man, is chiefly of archaic interest. He disputed some of Burke's account of the tussle between the French revolutionaries and the king and queen (always referring to his own good friend the Marquis de Lafayette by his title or 'nickname') and emphasized that if it were not for the arrogant rashness of the ruling house there would have been many of Lafayette's party willing to make a generous compromise. He dealt with the touchy question of public lynchings and beheadings, first by saying that there had been very few of them, and these conducted after great provocation, and second by saying that they paled in comparison with the hideous executions and tortures so lavishly indulged in by Europe's corrupt old monarchies. (He gave the especially lurid example of the dismemberment of Edmond Damiens, the very case later cited by Charles Dickens in *A Tale of Two Cities*.) Both Burke and Paine were writing before the Terror became real, and one cannot be certain whether Paine was arguing pre-emptively that violence would be justified if it did become expedient. He certainly did not foresee the exile and condemnation of his friend Lafayette, the hero of the American War of Independence. Much of what he wrote can be explained, if it cannot be defended, because it was composed during the period of 'dual power' in France, with apparently many more options and choices available.

Paine's claims, *contra* Burke, about the merits of the French Constitution, are likewise mainly of antique or ironic interest. He correctly pointed out that in England the qualifications for the franchise were absurd and anomalous as well as oppressive, and he emphasized that in France anyone paying taxes was (then) entitled to vote. It was to take him a little time to decide that there should be no property or financial qualification at all, while unlike Mary Wollstonecraft, who also replied to Burke, he was not a notable advocate of the rights of women, so he was not as far ahead of Burke's conservatism as he might have wished to be.

Paine's support for the idea of two-yearly elections for the National Assembly was something he came to regret, as we have seen, when it became applied to political control of the judiciary. Indeed, the Constitution's statement that 'Every community has a right to demand, of all its agents, an account of their conduct' could have struck him as ominous long before it actually did. (That claim of the right to an account is of course the perfect negation of Burke's address to his electors in Bristol.)

It was much easier for Paine to defend the ratio by which seats were apportioned as between the number of voters and the number of deputies, because the Britain of his time still endured the shame of the 'rotten borough' system, by which the hamlet of Old Sarum outvoted the city of Manchester, and was to continue to endure it until the 1832 Reform Act. In a related but not exactly similar way, the French repeal of game laws was in marked contrast to the equivalent feudal statutes in England, which denied the smallholder the right to the game on his own property and made it the property of the large landed proprietors.

Had there been no guillotine and no Bonaparte in the

immediate future of France, Paine's rebuke to Burke might have been studied to this day as a proof of the superiority of the Enlightenment and of radicalism over the hidebound attachment to tradition, faith and order. But Paine himself was uneasily aware that the counterposition was not as simple as that.

In reviewing one extremely important element of the argument about a new French Constitution, Paine implicitly quarrelled both with Burke and with the revolutionaries. His dislike for the privileges of the Church was adamant, but his model for a secular society remained an American one, as set out in Thomas Jefferson's Virginia Statute on Religious Freedom and as later enshrined in the First Amendment to the United States Constitution. By this precept, the state abstains from any arbitration in matters of the public establishment of religion, or in any matters of the private exercise of religious conscience. None of the state's tithes or taxes can be used for the support of any church. Its neutrality is absolute and unconditional. This *summa* of Enlightenment thought, developed in opposition to the old European twinship between Church and State and in particular to the establishment of a state church by the British Crown, was set out by Paine in *Rights of Man* in these words, and in fiery opposition to Burke's advocacy of state-sponsored piety:

> The inquisition in Spain does not proceed from the religion
> originally professed, but from this mule-animal, engendered

between the church and the state. The burnings in Smithfield proceeded from the same heterogenous production; and it was the regeneration of this strange animal in England afterwards, that renewed rancour and irreligion among the inhabitants, and that drove the people called Quakers and Dissenters to America. Persecution is not an original feature in *any* religion; but it is always the strongly-marked feature of all law-religions, or religions established by law. Take away the law-establishment, and every religion reassumes its original benignity. In America, a Catholic priest is a good citizen, a good character, and a good neighbour; an Episcopalian Minister is of the same description: and this proceeds, independently of the men, from there being no law establishment in America.[22]

One might pause here to note one mixed metaphor and one minor irony: the mule itself is incapable of reproduction so that for Paine's Church-State mating to have so many progeny the affection between the two partners must recur over several generations. And Mr Burke must surely have felt uncomfortable sometimes when defending an English 'church by law established' which did not recognize members of his own faith as true or loyal Christians.

However that might be, the French Revolution was bent, not upon dissociating the Church from the State, but upon nationalizing the Church and making it state property. At one early period, this took the form of a state-sponsored cult of the goddess 'Reason', who was to be adored and propitiated in special ceremonies to be held in, of all places, the Cathedral of Notre Dame. At other times, it was merely anti-clerical and confiscatory, while of course Bonaparte himself eventually took care to be crowned Emperor amid the usual crowds of priests and clouds of incense. The very Constitution praised by Paine grandly proclaimed 'The Nation' to be 'the source of all sovereignty', and some conservative historians have seen in this the seeds, not just of the Terror, but of modern totalitarian ideology in which the citizen himself is counted, in effect, as the property of the regime. To this day, the French state retains the right to appoint senior clergy: the precise opposite of the American system of strict neutrality as between state and religion, and between state and competing religions. This latter approach was praised by Paine in *Rights of Man*:

> With respect to what are called denominations of religion, if
> every one is left to judge of his own religion, there is no such
> thing as a religion that is wrong; but if they are to judge of
> each others religion, there is no such thing as a religion that
> is right; and therefore, all the world are right, or all the world
> are wrong.[23]

In a few simple sentences, he foreshadows all the disasters and crimes that have since attended every state that has tried to establish itself on the basis of theocracy. Yet when he speaks of France's Declaration of Rights, he is relatively mild in criticizing the relevant article – Article X – dealing with freedom of worship. Article X read as follows:

No man ought to be molested on account of his opinions, not even on account of his *religious* opinions, provided his avowal of them does not disturb the public order established by the law.[24]

Of this culpably vague formulation, Paine wrote that:

It is questioned by some very good people in France, as well as in other countries, whether the 10th article sufficiently guarantees the right it is intended to accord with: besides which, it takes off from the divine dignity of religion, and weakens its operative force upon the mind to make it a subject of human laws. It then presents itself to Man, like light intercepted from a cloudy medium, in which the source of it is obscured from his sight, and he sees nothing to reverence in the dusky ray.[25]

In a startlingly sentimental footnote to this observation, Paine expanded this point:

There is a single idea, which, if it strikes rightly upon the mind either in a legal or a religious sense, will prevent any man, or any body of men, or any government, from going wrong on the subject of religion; which is, that before any human institution of government were known in the world, there existed, if I may so express it, a compact between God and Man, from the beginning of time: and that as the relation and condition which man in his *individual person* stands in towards his Maker, cannot be changed, or any ways altered by any human laws or human authority, that religious devotion, which is a part of this compact, cannot so much as be made a subject of human laws; and that all laws must conform themselves to this prior existing compact, and not assume to make the compact conform to the laws, which, besides being human, are subsequent thereto. The first act of man, when he looked around and saw himself a creature which he did not make, and a world furnished for his reception, must have been devotion, and devotion must ever continue sacred to every individual man, *as it appears right to him*; and governments do mischief by interfering.[26]

It might not be strictly accurate to term this 'a single idea', but it does illustrate the importance that Paine – again like Burke – gave to the primeval origin of things, and to the precedents that might be derived from it. It also shows a definite generosity on his part where spiritual matters were concerned: he might speak of 'superstition' and 'priestcraft' but he did concede that humans were in some way innately religious. It foreshadows Marx's celebrated comments on religion in his critique of Hegel's philosophy of right, which is invariably misquoted with extreme vulgarity to make it appear as if Marx dismissed religion as 'the opium of the people'. What in fact he said was that religion expressed something eternal: 'the heart of a heartless world, the sigh of the oppressed creature, the spirit of a spiritless situation; the opiate of the people. Criticism has plucked the flowers from the chain, not so that men may wear the chain without consolation, but so that he may break the chain, and cull the living flower.' To both men, of course, it would have seemed grotesque by any definition to try and capture this numinous element of the human personality within the walls of any church, let alone a state-sponsored one.

The great achievement of Paine was to have introduced the discussion of *human* rights, and of their concomitant in democracy, to a large and often newly literate popular audience. Prior to this, discussion about 'rights' had been limited to 'natural' or 'civil' rights, and had been limited further to debates between philosophers. The dispute between Burke and Paine, indeed, is in part a replay of the disagreement between Thomas Hobbes and John Locke. Hobbes had written in his monumental *Leviathan* that

> The right of nature, which writers commonly call *Jus*
> *Naturale*, is the Liberty each man hath, to use his own power,
> as he will himself, for the preservation of his own Nature:
> that is to say of his own Life; and consequently of doing any
> thing, which in his own Judgment and Reason, he shall
> conceive to be the aptest means thereunto.[27]

Hobbes was well known for his fear of chaos and for his preoccupation with self-preservation and self-defence, which he believed necessary precisely to avoid the reversion to a state of nature in which every man would be for himself alone, so his reliance on both 'nature' and 'law' is problematic. But he matched his moral imperative for survival – which is only barely if at all a 'right' – with an obligation, or duty. In a rather ponderous version of the golden rule, he laid out the mutual duty like this:

> That a man be willing, when others are so too, as far forth as for Peace and defence of himself he may think it necessary, to lay down this right to all things; and be contented with so much liberty against other men, as he would allow other men against himself.[28]

This near-tautology leaves wide open the question of how it, or any other man-made agreement for mutual interest, can be held to emerge from any 'natural' order, and of how a law is to be distinguished from a right. It also leaves unresolved the issue of who is to decide, or arbitrate, or enforce. Rather uncertain as he was about the nature or existence of God, Hobbes postulated the necessity of a 'sovereign', who did not have to be an actual monarch, who would uphold or enforce those elements of contract to which he was not himself a party. This would take care of the recurrent and otherwise insoluble problem of an infinite number of human needs and desires, not all them satisfiable. 'Good and evil,' wrote Hobbes, 'are names that signify our appetites and aversions.' This formulation is nicely echoed by Paine when he writes, at the opening of *Common Sense*, that 'Society is produced by our wants, and government by our wickedness; the former promotes our happiness *positively* by uniting our affections, the latter *negatively* by restraining our vices.'

It is not known whether Paine ever read Hobbes, and he always denied having read John Locke's essay on 'Civil Government', but what he argued was in essence a more radical version of Locke's critique. Dissenting from the conclusions of *Leviathan*, Locke insists that the social contract is also binding on the sovereign. All governments, however derived, must be judged by the following standard:

> First: They are to govern by promulgated established laws, not to be varied in particular cases, to have one rule for rich and poor, for the favourite at Court, and the countryman at plough. Secondly: These laws also ought to be designed for no other end ultimately but the good of the people. Thirdly: They must not raise taxes on the property of the people without the consent of the people given by themselves or their deputies.[29]

(Paine was to say, in *Rights of Man*, concerning the House of Commons, that 'were [its] election as universal as taxation, which it ought to be, it would still be only the organ of the Nation'.) Locke added that lawmakers should never surrender their power to make law, 'or place it anywhere but where the people have'. It is easy to see the influence that the above essay, especially with its emphasis on taxation and representation, was to have on the drafting of the American

Declaration of Independence. Indeed, the 'dependence' on Locke is quite remarkable:

> Until the mischief be grown general, and the evil designs of the rulers become visible, the people, who are more disposed to suffer than to right themselves by resistance, are not apt to stir. [*Locke*]

> All experience hath shown, that mankind are more disposed to suffer, while evils are sufferable, than to right themselves by abolishing the forms to which they are accustomed. [*Declaration*]

> But if a long train of abuses, prevarications, and artifices, all tending the same way, make the design visible to the people, and they cannot but feel what they lie under and see whither they are going, it is not be wondered that they should then rouse themselves, and endeavour to put the rule into such hands which may secure to them the ends for which government was first erected. [*Locke*]

> But when a long train of abuses and usurpations, pursuing invariably the same course, evinces a design to reduce them under absolute despotism, it is their right, it is their duty to throw off such government, and to provide new guards for their future safety. [*Declaration*][30]

The Declaration actually went one crucial step further than Locke by taking his 'Life, liberty and property' and replacing it with a phrase that since has become much better known.

Like Burke's enemy Dr Price, Locke was an enthusiast of the 'Glorious Revolution' of 1688 and, like Price and Paine, he believed that it both could and did set a precedent for later rebellions should these become necessary. In his riposte to Hobbes, who did not allow for this challenge to the 'natural' order, he became sarcastic:

> As if when men, quitting the state of Nature, entered into Society, they agreed that all of them but one should be under the restraint of laws; but that he should still retain all the liberty of the state of Nature, increased with power, and made licentious by impunity. This is to think that men are so foolish that they take care to avoid what mischiefs may be done them by polecats or foxes, but are content, nay, think it safety, to be devoured by lions.[31]

The similarity of this passage to Paine's mordant observation on King William of Orange (page 72), is a very noticeable one.

There was an ethical dimension to the disagreement between Hobbes and Locke, not always made explicit, which concerned what we sometimes loosely call 'human nature'. Hobbes clearly felt that men left to themselves were liable to become selfish and brutal, and few will dispute that the empirical evidence for this is strong, to say the least. However, if 'society' is, so to speak, innate in mankind, then this must argue for the existence of an equally strong impulse for solidarity, for connection, and for mutual aid. Some have confused this with benevolence or idealism or even altruism, which is to miss the point. Civilization could never have arisen in any form if people had not been willing to subordinate their own ego to a general good, and it hardly matters if we decide that this concept of a general good is itself actuated partly by self-interest. Indeed, this point used to be central to the socialist ethos: both Wilde and Shaw were fond of maintaining that poverty and illness were an offence and a threat to the better-off, as well as to the poor or sick. Hume and Shaftesbury, two other thinkers of the Paine period, anticipated this by pointing out such obvious things as the readiness of strong men, who might have safely chosen to be selfish, to make sacrifices for their own families.

Thomas Paine did once pay some child support but was otherwise mostly without dependents. And he would not, I think, have been a socialist. He did not take the Levellers as his model (as David Hume had once done for the sake of argument). He admired enterprise and distrusted government, and often wrote of economic inequalities as if they were natural or inevitable. However, his own life experience, and his acquired contempt for the hereditary principle, meant he did not in the least believe that all unfairness or inequality was mandated. In Part Two of *Rights of Man* he put some practical flesh on the bones of his argument about human rights. In fact, he laid out the first design of a modern welfare state.

CHAPTER 4

Rights of Man, Part Two

Madame Roland may have been wrong when she said that Paine was more fit to scatter the kindling sparks than to lay the foundation, or 'better at lighting the way for revolution than drafting a constitution... or the day-to-day work of a legislator'. His personal history shows him to have been a good committee-man in more than one legislature in America and France. And there is a remarkable and much-overlooked passage, in the first part of *Rights of Man*, in which the great radical compared Burke, to his disadvantage, to the moral author of capitalism.

> Had Mr Burke possessed talents similar to the author of 'On The Wealth of Nations', he would have comprehended all the parts which enter into, and, by assemblage, form a constitution. He would have reasoned from minutiae to magnitude. It is not from his prejudices only, but from the disorderly cast of his genius, that he is unfitted for the subject he writes upon. Even his genius is without a constitution. It is a genius at random, and not a genius constituted. But he must say something. – He has therefore

mounted in the air like a balloon, to draw the eyes of the
multitude from the ground they stand upon.[1]

It is still more surprising that he expected his audience of artisans to know, and without even citing the author's name, who
and what he was talking about. But Adam Smith's book, published in the same year as the American Revolution, in fact had
a bracing effect on many radicals of the time. It argued against
mercantilist monopolies and against colonialism, as restraints
on free trade, and this of course recommended it very much in
Philadelphia. It also argued for rules, concerning contract, that
were intelligible and enforceable. This transparency was
vastly preferable, in rational eyes, to the system of semi-
magical authority so beloved by Burke. Remember also the
way in which Burke delivered his woebegone elegy for 'the
age of chivalry' and 'the glory of Europe'. It had been succeeded by the age of 'sophists, calculators and economists'.
Economists! One could hear him almost spitting the word. So
much for Adam Smith and his new-fangled Scots notions.

In the second part of *Rights of Man*, Paine set out, first,
to adumbrate the principles of constitutional government
and, second, to propose a system of social insurance. Part
Two was dedicated to the Marquis de Lafayette, who Paine
believed at that time would carry all before him as a French
revolutionary general. If we excuse this piece of romanticism,
we are dealing with a supremely realistic and businesslike
work, of which the two main chapters are plainly entitled 'Of
Constitutions' and 'Ways and Means'.

It might have been a desirable thing, wrote Paine, if human society had remained at a level and scale that would have permitted an Athenian model of government by direct participation. 'We see more to admire, and less to condemn, in that great, extraordinary people, than in anything which history affords.' (Under the heading of 'condemn' he did not specify whatever there may have been to condemn in the Athenian slave system.)

> As these democracies increased in population, and the territory extended, the simple democratical form became unwieldy and impracticable; and as the system of representation was not known, the consequence was, they either degenerated convulsively into monarchies, or became absorbed into such as then existed. Had the system of representation been then understood, as it now is, there is no reason to believe that those forms of government, now called monarchical or aristocratical, would ever have taken place.[2]

There is something slightly wrong with that last clause, and something very simplistic about the historical compression (as if civil war and class and religious and ethnic conflict had been omitted from the human story) but part of the point may be said to hold. No nation had managed to evolve a system of government that did not depend on some form of autocracy. This whole case was now altered by the American Revolution, which had bound itself and its heirs, in the name of the people, to certain inscribed rules and laws which no successor regime was allowed to break. Armed with this example, Paine declared that 'government without a constitution is power without a right'. He gave his readers a thorough account of the evolution of the United States Constitution, from the early days in Pennsylvania through the Continental Congress, the Declaration of Independence, the Articles of Confederation, the Constitutional Convention of 1787 and the gradual process by which every individual state had considered and then ratified the eventual document.

> Here we see a regular process – a government issuing out of
> a constitution, formed by the people in their original charac-
> ter; and that constitution serving, not only as an authority,
> *but as a law of control to the government.* [my italics][3]

The last point was exciting enough to Paine, and doubtless to many of his English readers, to deserve restatement and repetition. It perfectly exemplified his insistence on the original distinction to be made between state and society:

> There is no such thing as the idea of a compact between
> the people on one side, and the government on the other.
> The compact was that of the people with each other, to
> produce and constitute a government. To suppose that any
> government can be a party in a compact with the whole
> people, is to suppose it to have existence before it can have a
> right to exist.[4]

Paine went on, in order to draw an even more stark contrast with monarchy and heredity, to extol the figure of George Washington, as a man who had surrendered his commission as general when the war was ended, had been a private citizen holding no office when asked to preside over the Constitutional Convention, and only later become the country's president by free election. (Washington was to confirm this judgement of himself by indignantly refusing a petition from certain sycophantic officers to make himself king, and later by resigning the presidency without fuss to allow an electoral contest between John Adams and Thomas Jefferson.)

Paine went on to compare this self-generated self-government with the antiquated and corrupt state of affairs in England. In this he was not precisely comparing like with like. America – as we have seen, the very name 'America' had been used by English metaphysical poets to describe a new and untainted Eden, or a fresh lover – was an enterprise *de novo*, or *tabula rasa*. Thomas Jefferson, one of the founders of the American republic, preserved a letter from a French lady, the Comtesse de Houdetot, who reminded him of his good fortune in being able to begin afresh, rather than by having to pull down an ancient edifice and start among the ruins. Paine, moreover, did not mention the necessity of amending the US Constitution so as to set out a Bill of Rights. And he once again omitted to mention the persistence of slavery, which, by the Constitution's rating of a slave at the value of three-fifths of a citizen, was actually codified. However, he did succeed in showing that in England the acquisition of human rights, when they had been acquired at all, had been in the opposite direction: a process of *de haut en bas* in which the heirs of the Norman usurpers had made the occasional grudging concession. Magna Carta 'was no more than compelling the government to renounce a part of its assumptions', while William and Mary's so-called 'Bill of Rights' was 'but a bargain, which the parts of the government made with each other to divide powers, profits and privileges'. In speaking with further contempt of Magna Carta, and recalling again the tradition of popular rebellion, Paine wrote that if the barons were entitled to a memorial at Runnymede, surely Wat Tyler, murdered by treachery while trying to petition the king, deserved a monument in Smithfield.

Burke, by instinct, felt that this was all dangerous nonsense. Though it was not written down or in any way codified, the 1688 system of 'The Crown In Parliament' meant that the British already *had* a constitution. The Burkean mentality was very well caught by Charles Dickens's Mr Podsnap, in *Our Mutual Friend*, who even spoke in capitalized words upon the topic while condescending to a visiting Frenchman:

> Mr. Podsnap explained, with a sense of meritorious proprietorship. '… We Englishmen are Very Proud of Our Constitution, Sir. It was Bestowed Upon Us By Providence. No Other Country is so Favoured as This Country.'
>
> … 'And *other* countries,' said the foreign gentleman. 'They do how?'

'They do, Sir,' returned Mr Podsnap, gravely shaking his
head; 'they do – I am sorry to be obliged to say it – *as* they
do.'[5]

Taking a final swing at Burke, who had responded to the
first part of *Rights of Man* with the astonishingly supercilious
and perhaps minatory comment that the book should be left
to the system of 'criminal justice', Paine upbraided him for his
denial that governments were founded on the rights of men
and drew the conclusion that he must then believe that they
were founded on the rights of animals. After making this
somewhat tepid joke, he turned his attention to that other
great figure of counter-revolution, Dr Samuel Johnson.
Johnson could not see the need for any sort of written authority for government – he was of course a rank Tory, something
of a nostalgist for the Jacobite cause, and unlike Burke a
sworn foe of the mutinous and ungrateful American colonists
– and so Paine undertook to enlighten him. His ostensible
proposal was for a constitution, apparently on the American
model he so admired, but with two rather noticeable differences.

In order to forestall any revival or recurrence of
Hanoverian-style autocracy, the Founding Fathers at
Philadelphia had insisted on the most elaborate separation of
powers. Famously, these consisted of the division of adminis-
tration, like Caesar's Gaul, into three parts: the legislature, the
executive, and the judiciary. Two houses would act as a check
on any sudden or short-term electoral enthusiasm, and the

courts as a restraint on the executive. Paine did not see the necessity of separating the legislature and the judiciary, and professed to believe that there was only one important division – 'that of legislating or enacting laws, and that of executing or administering them'. (As we have seen, he was to rapidly alter this opinion when confronted with majoritarian bullying in the French Assembly.)

Paine also opposed the concept of two 'houses' for the passage of legislation, and favoured a unicameral parliament. (He had made the same recommendation in *Common Sense* during the American revolution, to the great ire of John Adams, who never forgave him for it.) Of the bicameral system it could not be 'proved', he said, 'on the principles of just representation, that either should be wiser or better than the other.' That may well have been true, and could still be true, but the principle is the same – that no sudden rush of passion or prejudice should overwhelm the legislature without the chance of a review or a reconsideration. Paine seemed to concede this very point, when he proposed a division by lot of the single house into three segments that would individually debate any proposed bill before reuniting for a final and deciding vote. Along with his proposal for triannual elections and the replacement of one third of parliament's membership every year, this quasi-utopian scheme seems also to have been subjected to revision in his mind after his experience in France. It survives to this day, in the effort to discipline or restrain elected representatives by means of 're-selection' in Britain or 'term limitation' in the United States.

(It also affords, if one ignores the limited electorate of the time and the existence of a hereditary house of peers, an almost perfect contrast with Edmund Burke's *Letter* to the electors of Bristol, which insists that a member is not a delegate.)

The next stage of Part Two of *Rights of Man* shows Paine to be an early supporter of free enterprise and social democracy, as well as a bit of a utilitarian. He proposes, in words that Adam Smith could have approved, that empire is foolish because 'the expense of maintaining dominion more than absorbs the profit of any trade'. He points out, in terms that John Maynard Keynes could also have approved, that war and conquest in Europe were likewise futile, since the ruin of another country will inevitably help to bankrupt one's own. 'When the ability in any nation to buy is destroyed, it equally involves the seller.' That phrase might encapsulate Keynes's *Economic Consequences of the Peace*. Finally, Paine insists in straight Benthamite terms that 'Whatever the form or constitution of government might be, it ought to have no other object than the *general* happiness'.

In his exaltation of commerce and free trade over feudalism, he not only seconded Adam Smith and anticipated the later classical school, but also anticipated Karl Marx, who viewed capitalism as a revolutionary force that would tear traditional obedience and hierarchy to shreds. In a celebrated piece of what we might call ancient English deference, Burke had written stirringly of the great estates and their proprietors, and their claim to be the guarantors of 'manly, moral, regulated liberty'. As opposed to this rural grandeur, what were the radicals but a noisome pest?

> Because half a dozen grasshoppers under a fern make the
> field ring with their importunate chink, while thousands of
> great cattle, reposed beneath the shadow of the British oak,
> chew the cud and are silent, pray do not imagine that those
> who make the noise are the only inhabitants of the field... or
> that, after all, they are other than the little shrivelled,
> meagre, hopping, though loud and troublesome insects of
> the hour.[6]

Paine had nothing but impatience with this sneering
assertion of rustic stability, of the sort which used to be a
centrepiece of the Tory imagery of 'the shires', and he had an
insect metaphor of his own. It was absurd for Burke to speak
of 'the pillar of the landed interest':

> Were that pillar to sink into the earth, the same landed prop-
> erty would continue, and the same ploughing, sowing and
> reaping would go on. The aristocracy are not the farmers
> who work the land, and raise the produce, but are the mere
> consumers of the rent; and when compared with the active
> world are the drones, a seraglio of males, who neither
> collect the honey nor form the hive, but exist only for lazy
> enjoyment.[7]

This took up the traditional cry of the English radical,
which was to endure from Wat Tyler to the days of Lloyd
George, that the land could self-evidently not be the product
of any one class's genius or otherwise, but was instead the

common means by which all could make a living. It was notorious that hardship and poverty were widespread in rural
areas, where the means to feed and clothe and nurture many
people already existed. Rebecca West once observed that one
of the great failures of human civilization has been its refusal
to pay proper attention, or a proper wage, to those who
perform the hard but essential primary task of growing our
food. Paine did not propose anything on the order of national-
ization or collectivization, but he did advance a plan for the
amelioration of poverty and want.

Painstaking, charted and laid out in statistical tables, it
showed that his time as an excise-man had not been wasted.
But, these pages are now rather tedious to read, because they
take the then-current estimates of population, and because
they calculate government taxes and revenues and outgoings
in the monetary values that then obtained. All we need to
know is that Paine proposed the abolition of the existing Poor
Laws, and their replacement by: provision for two hundred
and fifty-two thousand poor families; education for one
million and thirty thousand children; comfortable provision
for one hundred and forty thousand aged persons; donations
of twenty shillings each for fifty thousand births and donations of twenty shillings each for twenty thousand marriages.[8]

It can be seen that Paine had thought of the concept of
'cradle to grave', or 'womb to tomb' coverage and had also
conceived of it as a 'right'. But he did not concern himself with
health insurance. He may have thought that giving people
the ability to pay a physician was enough: at all events his

preoccupation was more with emancipating people from crushing need than with awarding them a 'safety net'. There was also a question of right. Those who had worked hard all their lives were not to be cast away when their muscles and brains softened, and those born into a hard life should not be readied only for the scrap-heap. His opinions on this were to become more advanced: in a later pamphlet entitled *Agrarian Justice* Paine proposed that a certain sum be given, as a one-time assurance of a start in life, to anyone of either sex reaching the age of majority. To pay for all this he proposed a graduated and very modest income tax, and a duty to be paid on death.

One more observation must be made on the forward-looking character of *Rights of Man*. Paine believed that quarrels between nations, as well as within nations, were occasioned by monarchies. He also believed that the increase in manufacturing, trade and technological innovation would tend to make nations more pacific. However, he was not so naïve as to believe that war and aggression would become things of the past. He boldly proposed that America, France and England, together with the Dutch, form a federation for naval disarmament, based on mutual reductions in the size of their fleets, and then impose their programme upon the other European empires. Most notably, he suggested that 'the above confederated powers' would be able to persuade Spain to allow 'the independence of South America, and the opening of those countries of immense extent and wealth to the general commerce of the world, as North America now is'.

RIGHTS OF MAN | 122

He was later to revisit this point in proposing an 'Association of Nations for the Rights and Commerce of Nations': quite possibly the first prefiguration of the League of Nations and subsequently the UN.

With this mixture of sober practicality and sublime optimism, Paine summarized his case:

> Never did so great an opportunity offer itself to England,
> and to all Europe, as is produced by the two Revolutions of
> America and France. By the former, freedom has a national
> champion in the Western world; and by the latter, in Europe.
> When another nation shall join France, despotism and bad
> government will scarcely dare to appear. To use a trite
> expression, the iron is becoming hot all over Europe. The
> insulted German and the enslaved Spaniard, the Russ and
> the Pole, are beginning to think. The present age will here-
> after merit to be called the Age of reason…[9]

CHAPTER 5

The Age of Reason

A proper discussion of *Rights of Man* would be unfinished without some mention of *The Age of Reason*, which is in a sense its counterpart and completion. Paine himself implied as much in the last sentence quoted at the end of the previous chapter, as he did in the short preface he subjoined to his dedication to *The Age of Reason* itself, which was 'To My Fellow Citizens of the United States of America'.

> You will do me the justice to remember, that I have always strenuously supported the Right of every Man to his own opinion, however different that opinion might be to mine. He who denies to another this right, makes a slave of himself to his present opinion, because he precludes himself the right of changing it.
>
> The most formidable weapon against errors of every kind is Reason. I have never used any other, and I trust I never shall.[1]

The first of these paragraphs is as pithy a statement of the case for unconditional freedom of expression as has been made since John Milton published his *Areopagitica*. The second is slightly disingenuous. Paine had by no means always relied upon pure reason as his method of argument. Indeed, throughout the pages of *Common Sense*, *The Crisis* and even *Rights of Man*, he made continuous use of scriptural authority. He knew very well that the Bible was the only book he could count on many of his audience having read, and he did not hesitate, for example, to claim that monarchy is discredited by the Old Testament – which, as is usual with that volume, it is in some passages, while being authorized in others.

The publishing history of *The Age of Reason* is even more interesting than the series of risks and chances that attended the birth of *Rights of Man*. In the spring of 1793, feeling himself increasingly threatened by the approach of Robespierre's police, Paine sat himself down in his lodgings in St Denis to write an account of his attitude towards religion. A version of it – which is to say, a version of Part One of *The Age of Reason* – was printed in Paris in March 1793, entitled *Le Siècle de la Raison, ou Le Sens Commun des Droits de l'Homme*. The French title further demonstrates the way in which Paine regarded it as the culmination of his previous works. Only one incomplete copy of this edition has come down to us, and it has no author's name on the title-page.

As the year wore on, Paine evidently felt that he might have little time left in which to give his full opinion on the subject. He accordingly revised and extended the book, and was celebrating its completion in late December 1793 when the revolutionary cops banged on his door and took him away to the Luxembourg prison. He had just time to hand the manuscript to his American friend Joel Barlow.

There is no doubt that Paine had long desired to explain why he was not a Christian. John Adams, who never trusted him, had been disconcerted in 1776 to hear him express 'a contempt of the Old Testament, and indeed of the Bible at large'. But by 1793 there was another pressing motive for a proper account. Paine wanted to prevent the French Revolution from becoming a full-blown instatement of atheism. Much as he may have welcomed the end of the rotten alliance between pulpit and throne, he was dismayed by the violent rush towards godlessness. His book, therefore, had the dual purpose of subverting organized religion and asserting 'deism'.

It is perhaps a testimony to the state of affairs in France at that date that Paine did not even have access to a bible when he was composing Part One of *The Age of Reason*. But he knew the book well enough by heart to make very few mistakes, and was able to continue revising the work in this way while he lay in his dank cell. Upon his release, he was taken in by Ambassador James Monroe and his wife, and in their home was furnished with a bible. Part Two was finished by October 1795. It is somewhat arresting to think of a book being begun by candlelight by a hunted dissident, then updated from memory in a death cell, and finally completed in the home of a distinguished future president of the United States.

The opening paragraphs of the book consist of a

'profession of faith', as Paine candidly called it, and are obviously somewhat modelled on the Athanasian or Nicene 'creeds':

> I believe in one God, and no more; and I hope for happiness beyond this life.
>
> I believe in the equality of man, and I believe that religious duties consist in doing justice, loving mercy, and endeavouring to make our fellow creatures happy...
>
> I do not believe in the creed professed by the Jewish church, by the Roman church, by the Greek church, by the Turkish church, by the Protestant church, nor by any church that I know of. My own mind is my own church.
>
> All national institutions of churches, whether Jewish, Christian, or Turkish, appear to me no other than human inventions set up to terrify and enslave mankind, and monopolize power and profit.[2]

This recalls the old joke about how Unitarians believe in one god at the very most, or the related joke (from the American novelist Peter De Vries, who was raised in a Dutch Reformed family in Chicago) that the evolution of theology, from polytheism to only one God, is getting nearer and nearer to the correct figure.

But Paine was not joking in the least. He shared with the religious a belief that the handiwork of God was all about us, attested by the order and beauty of the natural world. (In a generous moment near the end of the book, Paine directed his

readers to Edmund Burke's essay 'On the Sublime and the
Beautiful', as showing a more proper appreciation of our sur-
roundings.) He himself put it like this:

> It is only in the CREATION that all our ideas and concep-
> tions of a *word of God* can unite. The creation speaketh an
> universal language, independently of human speech or
> human language, multiplied and various as they be. It is an
> ever existing original, which every man can read. It cannot
> be forged; it cannot be counterfeited; it cannot be lost; it
> cannot be altered; it cannot be suppressed. It does not
> depend upon the will of man whether it shall be published
> or not; it publishes itself from one end of the earth to the
> other.[3]

That was his riposte to the claim of 'revelation', as made by
Mosaic and Christian and Muslim authorities (all of whom, of
course, claimed the revelation for their own). Such reported
words of God, wrote Paine, could originally only be hearsay
at best, and then be the property of an interpreting priesthood. Yet an actual revelation was within the scope of any
thinking or feeling person, and was offered with natural generosity, and (a small but important point) did not depend on
whether you spoke Hebrew, or Arabic, or Greek or Latin, or
whether you would have to wait for, or indeed trust in, the
priestly translation.[4]

Flowery as Paine's naturalism may appear, it expresses his
very decided view that all other arguments for the existence

RIGHTS OF MAN | 128

of God were indeed based on human forgeries or, at best, human improvisations. Taking the Bible chapter by chapter, he noticed what many people have noticed for themselves both before and since: that it is shot through with absurdity, inconsistency and immorality, and that it borrows its images wholesale from previously existing mythologies. To begin, as it were, at the beginning:

> The Christian mythologists, after having confined Satan in a pit, were obliged to let him out again, to bring on the sequel of the fable. He is then introduced into the garden of Eden in the shape of a snake, or a serpent, and in that shape he enters into familiar conversation with Eve, who is in no way surprised to hear a snake talk; and the issue of this tête-à-tête is, that he persuades her to eat an apple, and the eating of that apple damns all mankind.[5]

If Paine had been able to have his Bible open beside him at that point, he might have checked and found that, though tempters are indeed often represented as the Evil One, the snake in Genesis is not in fact described as a personification of Satan. None the less, and even without this detail, the story is as foolish as it could possibly be. It further represents God as a capricious and insecure person, whose plans can be undone by one of the lowest of his creation, and who fashions human beings only in order to torment and worry them.

Pressing along through the prophets, Paine comes to Isaiah's famous line: 'Behold, a virgin shall conceive, and bear a son', and has no difficulty in demonstrating that, in context, this is a promise to Ahaz, King of Judah, that this very sign will give him victory over the kings of Syria and Israel. Not only is the old Hebrew word for 'virgin' quite often used as a synonym for 'nubile woman', but the promise of the birth is fulfilled within the limits of the story itself. However, we later discover in the book of Chronicles that the prophecy did Ahaz no good at all, since he lost the war and saw his people massacred and enslaved in the manner so often described with such relish throughout the Old Testament.

But even if the prophecy of Isaiah was supposed to apply to the later birth of Jesus of Nazareth, Paine has no trouble in showing that all accounts of the virgin birth are ludicrous and internally inconsistent. Indeed, he demonstrates by means of mathematical computation and genealogical graphs that either all four of the apostles, Matthew, Mark, Luke and John, were liars or else they were quarrelling very damningly among themselves. At none of the crucial points can they make their stories agree, whether it is the crucifixion or the ascension into heaven, and it is plain that they were not themselves witnesses to anything that they purported to describe. Everything 'happened' years before the writers were born. For Paine, this consummates the basically fictional character of the preceding Old Testament, in which the 'authors' consistently refer to things that occurred, if they occurred at all, long after the supposed writers had died. (One or other delusion or fabrication, as you might say, but not both.)

Paine's close textual reading is still impressive after all

these years, when we have grown easily accustomed to the village atheist who can triumphantly ask: 'Where did Cain get his wife?' I was myself, after long practice at this, rather amazed to discover how many other children the Virgin Mary, according to Matthew 8: 55–56, seems to have had. There are some errors of fact: Jesus if he existed would have spoken Aramaic and not Hebrew. There are some unfairnesses: Peter's terrified renunciation of his lord does not deserve to be called 'perjury'. It is not really true to say that Jesus has only to die to make his point: he has to be rejected and then painfully killed. So Paine's literal-minded reductionism sometimes lets him down. He also cannot decide whether the supposed preachings of the Nazarene are admirable or not. In general, he follows the custom of most deists in rating the sermons and maxims as moral and 'amiable'. Yet he cannot conceal his contempt for the most central tenet of Christianity, which is the morally hideous concept of scapegoating or 'vicarious atonement':

> If I owe a person money, and cannot pay him, and he threatens to put me in prison, another person can take the debt upon himself and pay it for me. But if I have committed a crime, every circumstance of the case is changed. Moral justice cannot take the innocent for the guilty even if the innocent would offer itself. To suppose justice to do this, is to destroy the principle of its existence, which is the thing itself. It is then no longer justice. It is indiscriminate revenge.[6]

In other words, to hope to throw your sins upon another, especially if this involves a human sacrifice, is a grotesque evasion of moral and individual responsibility.

Divided as he was between wishing to show religion as immoral, and belief in God as simultaneously essential, Paine was somewhat disposed to split some important differences. His belief that the natural and cosmological order implied a creator – this is commonly known as 'the argument from design' – had been refuted as a fallacy by Immanuel Kant some time before. Paine would most probably never have heard of Kant, whose work did not appear in English until the mid-nineteenth century, and A. J. Ayer further says that there is no evidence that he ever read David Hume. This slightly astonishes me, because here is Paine on miracles:

> If we are to suppose a miracle to be something so entirely
> out of the course of what is called nature, that she must go
> out of that course to accomplish it; and we see an account
> given of such miracle by a person who said he saw it, it
> raises a question in the mind very easily decided, which is: Is
> it more probable that nature should go out of her course, or
> that a man should tell a lie?[7]

And here is Hume on miracles, in his *Enquiry Concerning Human Understanding*, which was published in 1748:

> No testimony is sufficient to establish a miracle, unless the

testimony be of such a kind that its falsehood would be more miraculous than the fact that it endeavours to establish.[8]

With part of his mind, Paine was probably contending with the Bishop of Llandaff, who had written a book to demonstrate to his own satisfaction that the status of the rich and the poor was determined by God as part of the natural order. Even as late as my own childhood, the Church of England hymnal included as one verse in 'All Things Bright and Beautiful':

> The rich man in his castle
> The poor man at his gate
> God made them high and lowly
> And ordered their estate.

The same bishop also wrote a vindication of, or 'Apology For', the Bible, in which he did make a few concessions to what Paine had asserted. He was willing to admit that Moses could not have written all of the Pentateuch and that David was not invariably the Psalmist. But he would not give too much ground. Paine was quite out of order, wrote the good bishop, in saying that God had ordered the slaughter of all adult male and female Midianites, preserving only the daughters for rapine. On the contrary, the daughters had been preserved solely for the purpose of slavery. No hint of immorality was involved.

This example alone will serve to remind us that *The Age of*

Reason belongs to the prehistory of the argument, as indeed does deism. Paine does not tell us this, but the belief of many original deists was not unlike that of Dr Pangloss in Voltaire's *Candide*, that 'all is for the best in the best of all possible worlds'. There could be no question of free will in a globe that was already complete and had been fully stocked and furnished. Mankind was in some ways just as capriciously treated as he would be if he were Job, with the exception that his creator had made him and then forgotten or abandoned him. Not even flat-out atheist materialism offered such a bleak picture. But of course flat-out atheism was barely imaginable in the decades just before the publication of *The Origin of Species*, with its altogether more plausible explanation of our beginnings.

Paine was an engineer and amateur scientist, and stood on tiptoe to see as far as he could over the existing horizon. He half-understood the concept of infinity and of the infinite plurality of possible other galaxies, but he could not leave hold of the idea that this made the terrestrial globe much more unique, rather than quite possibly less, and he could not fail to find what he sought, which was the role of a 'Creator' in the process. However, at least he did not think that this creator was a lunatic or a sadist. Those who look up the pages of *The Age of Reason* may find themselves slightly jolted by the abrupt manner in which Paine employs the term 'the Jews'. I do not myself think that he intended to criticize any but the adherents of stern Judaism, because prejudice against the Jews has a habit of breaking out anywhere in a person afflicted with it, and there is no hint of it anywhere else in Paine's work. I would also cite this passage as evidence:

> A man is preached instead of a God; an execution as an object for gratitude; the preachers daub themselves with the blood like a troop of assassins and pretend to admire the brilliancy it gives them. They preach a hum-drum sermon on the merits of the execution; praise Jesus Christ for being executed; and condemn the Jews for doing it.[9]

On 8 June 1809, Thomas Paine died. On 12 February of the same year, Charles Darwin and Abraham Lincoln had been born. These two emancipators of humanity – Darwin the greatest – were in different ways to complete and round off the arguments that Paine had helped to begin.

Paine's Legacy

It is commonly believed that Paine's last years in America were a time of squalor and bitterness and decline, eventuating in a pauper's grave and in the total eclipse of his reputation. This, like most half-truths, is not 50 per cent true so much as it is quite misleading. To be sure, Paine had isolated himself and alienated many old friends. He was determined to get even with his former hero, George Washington, for example, who he felt had abandoned him in his time of need in Robespierre's terrorized Paris. There may have been grounds for his believing this, but he went on to say that Washington had been of little use in the original Revolutionary War, which was an opinion he might more bravely or consistently have advanced at the time.

He also sacrificed many former comrades by his publication of *The Age of Reason*. Even Dr Benjamin Rush, companion of his early days in Philadelphia, refused on that account to speak to him anymore. Some may have felt the book to be irreligious, which it plainly was not, but others may have felt, again, that if this was the way Paine truly felt about the Bible he should have said so earlier, rather than using it as a textual prop when it suited him.

In addition, Paine, who had never been extremely fastidious about his dress or his appearance, was by many accounts running rather drastically to seed. His health had been almost shattered by the confinement in the Luxembourg prison, and his face had become inflamed and blotchy. This 'look' made it easy for his enemies to circulate the story that he was a hopeless drunk and, though there are few if any accounts of him as actually inebriated to the point of incapacity, there is no doubt that he had recourse to the bottle.

It must also be admitted that he never gave up his hope that Britain would lose the war with France. Nelson's victory at Trafalgar in October 1805 he regarded as an event overstated by the press. He still made occasional fond remarks about Bonaparte, even after his coronation as Emperor.

However, he was to continue to make himself useful in several ways. His mere physical presence, as the original trumpet of the American Revolution, helped to put heart into the anti-Federalist forces led by Thomas Jefferson, who were at that time recovering from the persecution they had suffered under John Adams's notorious 'Alien and Sedition Acts'. This combat was of some importance, because although the Federalist and Whig and Republican parties no longer exist in their original forms, the development of a party system required some clear separations on points of principle.

Paine saw what was happening to the Indians, and saw also that the theft of their land and the threat to their existence came largely from proselytizing Christianity, which was used as a hypocritical cover for greed. After the New York Missionary Society had staged a meeting with the leaders of the Osage Indians in order, or so they said, to present them with a copy of the Bible, Paine asked sarcastically what good this was intended to do:

> Will they [the Osage Indians] learn sobriety and decency
> from drunken Noah and beastly Lot; or will their daughters
> be edified by the examples of Lot's daughter? Will not the
> shocking accounts of the destruction of the Canaanites when
> the Israelites invaded their country, suggest the idea that we
> may serve them in the same manner, or the accounts stir
> them up to do the like to our people on the frontiers, and
> then justify the assassination by the bible the Missionaries
> have given them?[1]

It can be seen from the above, incidentally, that while Paine was indignant at the cheating of the Indians he did not at all romanticize them. Indeed, he always remained a very practical man. He thought he saw a huge opening for American diplomacy when his once-admired Napoleon got into financial difficulties. On Christmas Day 1802, he wrote to President Jefferson:

> Spain has ceded Louisiana to France, and France has
> excluded the Americans from N. Orleans and the navigation
> of the Mississippi: the people of the Western Territory have

complained of it to their Government, and the government is of consequence involved in and interested in the affair. The question then is – what is the best step to be taken?…
Suppose the Government begin by making a proposal to France to repurchase the cession, made to her by Spain, of Louisiana, provided it be with the consent of the people of Louisiana or a majority thereof… The French treasury is not only empty, but the Government has consumed by anticipation a great part of the next year's revenue. A monied proposal will, I believe, be attended to; if it should, the claims upon France can be stipulated as part of the payments, and that sum can be paid here to the claimants.

I congratulate you on the *birthday of the New Sun*, now called Christmas-day, and I make you a present of a thought on Louisiana.[2]

This bold letter, with its boldly secular concluding salutation, was in its way a settling of the imbalance as between the American and French Revolutions, settling it very much in the favour of the United States. Jefferson had been thinking along the same lines himself, and was eventually to make the greatest land-deal in history by doubling the size of the USA at the cost of ten cents an acre, while gaining control of the Mississippi. From then on, the future of the United States as a continental and thus as a world power was assured. Paine, of course, always hoped that this would be a superpower for liberty and democracy, and he was to suffer an immediate and shocking disappointment. Jefferson allowed the continuing importation of slaves into the new territories. In the long run, this meant an expansion of the number of slave states as opposed to free ones, and thus made it certain that there would one day be a civil war. In the shorter run, it was a glaring injustice. Paine and Joel Barlow attempted to change Jefferson's mind, urging him to settle thrifty German immigrants in the new lands and to permit black families to travel from other states to acquire their own land there, but the sugar interest triumphed, as had the cotton interest in other states, and once again the chance to cleanse America of its original stain was missed.

Paine's closing years, pitiful as they were, contained one closing triumph. He might have become a scarecrow-like figure. He might have been forced to subsist on the charity of friends. He might have been denied the right to vote by a bullying official, when presenting himself at the polling station, on the grounds that the author of *Common Sense* was not a true American. But as the buzzards began to circle, he rallied one more time. It was widely believed by the devout of those days that unbelievers would scream for a priest when their own death-beds loomed. Why this was thought to be valuable propaganda it is impossible to say. Surely the sobbing of a human creature *in extremis* is testimony not worth having, as well as testimony extracted by the most contemptible means? Boswell had been to visit David Hume under these conditions, because he had been reluctant to believe that the stoicism of the old philosopher would hold up, and as a result we have one excellent account of the refusal of the intelligence to yield to such moral blackmail. Our other account comes from those who attended Paine. Dying in ulcerated agony, he was imposed upon by two Presbyterian ministers who pushed past his housekeeper and urged him to avoid damnation by accepting Jesus Christ. 'Let me have none of your Popish stuff,' Paine responded. 'Get away with you, good morning, good morning.' The same demand was made of him as his eyes were closing. 'Do you wish to believe that Jesus Christ is the son of God?' He answered quite distinctly: 'I have no wish to believe on that subject.' Thus he expired with his reason, and his rights, both still staunchly defended until the very last.

In the year 1798, seeking to choke the influence of French and other revolutionary opinions in their own 'backyard', the British authorities jailed the radical Irish nationalist Arthur O'Connor. As he was being led away, O'Connor handed out a poem of his own composition that seemed to its readers like a meek act of contrition, and a repudiation of that fount of heresy, Thomas Paine:

> The pomp of courts and pride of kings
> I prize above all earthly things;
> I love my country; the king
> Above all men his praise I sing:
> The royal banners are displayed,
> And may success the standard aid.

> I fain would banish far from hence,
> The Rights of Man and Common Sense;
> Confusion to his odious reign,
> That foe to princes, Thomas Paine!
> Defeat and ruin seize the cause
> Of France, its liberties and laws![3]

If the reader will have the patience to take a pencil, and take the first line of the first stanza, and then the first line of the second stanza, and then repeat the alternating process with the second, third and fourth lines of each, and so on, he or she will have no difficulty in writing out quite a different poem. (How much the British have suffered from their fatuous belief that the Irish are stupid!)

So it has gone with the work and reputation of Thomas Paine: sometimes obscure, and sometimes a mere figure in the carpet, and at other times standing out in bold and salient letters. It was even the case with his poor cadaver. That eccentric English radical and scribbler, William Cobbett, who had been for years a vicious critic of Paine, underwent a change of heart and removed his skeleton for reburial in England. A macabre chapter of accidents was the result, and for years there were bids for a skull here, a rib there: something that Paine with his detestation of relics and cults would have entirely deplored. He would certainly have agreed with his friend Joel Barlow that his own writings were his best memorial.

As the nineteenth century progressed, Paine's inspiration resurfaced, and his influence was felt in the movement for reform of Parliament in England, and in the agitation against slavery in America. John Brown, ostensibly a Calvinist, had Paine's books in his camp. Abraham Lincoln was a close reader of his work, and used to deploy arguments from *The Age of Reason* in his disputes with religious sectarians, as well as more general Paineite themes in his campaign to turn a bloody Civil War into what he called 'a second American revolution'. The later rise of the Labour movement, and the agitation for women's suffrage, all saw Paine's example being revived and quoted. When Franklin Roosevelt made his great speech to rally the American people against fascism after the attack on Pearl Harbor, he quoted an entire paragraph from Paine's *Crisis*, beginning: 'These are the times that try men's souls…'

No president was to call upon Paine again until Ronald Reagan tried to enlist him in a quasi-libertarian campaign to reduce the size of government and to take on the moribund Soviet empire. 'We have it in our power,' said the old man, picking up one of Paine's more dubious statements, 'to begin the world over again.' This sort of emulation and plagiarism is a very particular kind of flattery, because it promotes Paine's work to that exalted company shared by the Bible and the works of Shakespeare, which recur to the mind in times of stress, or of need, or even of joy. In a time when both rights and reason are under several kinds of open and covert attack, the life and writing of Thomas Paine will always be part of the arsenal on which we shall need to depend.

NOTES

Please note that all citations for Thomas Paine's work are taken from the Library of America edition, Literary Classics of the US, 1995 New York.

Introduction

1 Thomas Paine, *Rights of Man*, p. 443.
2 Thomas Paine, *Rights of Man, Part Two*.
3 Thomas Paine, *Rights of Man, Part One*, pp. 434–5.
4 Ibid., pp. 442–3.

Chapter 1

1 John Keane, *Tom Paine: A Political Life*, London, Bloomsbury, 1996, p. 84.
2 Ibid.
3 'African Slavery in America' *Pennsylvania Journal and Weekly Advertiser*, 8 March 1775.
4 John Keane, *Tom Paine: A Political Life*, London, Bloomsbury, 1996, p. 103.
5 Ibid.
6 Thomas Paine, *Common Sense*, p. 23.
7 C. R. C. Fletcher and Rudyard Kipling, 'The American Rebellion and the Great French War 1760–1815; Reign of George III' *A

History of England, 1911, New York, Doubleday, p. 239.

8   Thomas Paine, *Common Sense*, p. 36.

9   Thomas Paine, *The American Crisis, I*, p. 91.

10 Ibid., p. 95.

11 Ibid., p. 96.

12 Thomas Paine, *The American Crisis, II*, p. 109.

13 Harvey J. Kaye, *Thomas Paine and the Promise of America*, New York, Hill and Wang, 2005, p. 65.

Chapter 2

1   Conor Cruise O'Brien, *The Great Melody*, Chicago, University of Chicago Press, 1992.

2   John Keane, *Tom Paine: A Political Life*, London, Bloomsbury, 1996, p. 451.

Chapter 3

1   Conor Cruise O'Brien, *The Long Affair*, Chicago, University of Chicago Press, 1998, p. 102.

2   Conor Cruise O'Brien, *The Great Melody*, Chicago, University of Chicago Press, 1992, p. 597.

3   John Keane, *Tom Paine: A Political Life*, London, Bloomsbury, 1996, p. 292.

4   Edmund Burke, as quoted in Conor Cruise O'Brien's, *Edmund Burke*, London, Random House, 1997, p. 219–220.

5   Ibid., p. 217.

6   Ibid., p. 221.

7   ibid.

8   ibid.

9   ibid.

10 Burke's *Reflections on the Revolution in France*, London, Macmillan, 1890.

11 Ibid.

12 Thomas Paine, *Rights of Man, Part One*, p. 438.

13 Ibid., p. 438.

14 Ibid., p. 487.

15 Ibid., pp. 487–8.

16 Ibid., p. 461.

17 Ibid., p. 464.

18 Ibid., pp. 476–7.

19 Ibid., p. 480.

20 Ibid., p. 466.

21 Ibid., p. 467.

22 Ibid., p. 484.

23 Ibid., p. 483.

24 Ibid., p. 507.

25 Ibid., p. 508.

26 Ibid., pp. 508–9, footnote.

27 Thomas Hobbes, *Leviathan*, London, J. M. Dent & Sons, 1914, p. 66.

28 Ibid., p. 67.

29 A. J. Ayer, *Thomas Paine*, London, Secker & Warburg, 1988, p. 17.

30 A. Owen Aldridge, *Thomas Paine's American Ideology*, Newark, University of Delaware Press, p. 122.

31 A. J. Ayer, *Thomas Paine*, London, Secker & Warburg, 1988, p. 17.

Chapter 4

1 Thomas Paine, *Rights of Man, Part Two*, p. 472.

2 Ibid., p. 565.

3 Ibid., p. 574.

4 Ibid., p. 575.

5 Charles Dickens *Our Mutual Friend*, London, David Campbell Publishers Ltd., 1994, p. 133.

6   John Keane, *Tom Paine: A Political Life*, London, Bloomsbury, 1996, p. 293.

7   Thomas Paine, *Rights of Man, Part Two*, p. 612.

8   Ibid., p. 642.

9   Ibid., p. 652.

Chapter 5

1   Thomas Paine, *The Age of Reason*, p. 665.

2   Ibid., p. 666.

3   Ibid., p. 687.

4   In Part Two of *The Age of Reason*, Paine may have intended a small satire on Burke when he wrote, concerning the unbelievable miracles of Joshua, that 'the sublime and the ridiculous are so often so nearly related that it is difficult to class them seperately.' As for as I am aware, this is the first use of this famous contrast. Thomas Paine, *The Age of Reason*, p. 751.

5   Ibid., p. 672.

6   Thomas Paine, *The Age of Reason*, p. 685.

7   Ibid., p. 715.

8   David Hume, *Enquiry Concerning Human Understanding*, Oxford, Oxford University Press, 1999, p. 174.

9   Thomas Paine, *The Age of Reason*, p. 825.

Conclusion

1   John Keane, *Tom Paine: A Political Life*, London, Bloomsbury, 1996, p. 499.

2   Christopher Hitchens, *Thomas Paine: The Actuarial Radical*, Grand Street, Autumn 1987.

3   I am indebted to R. B. Bernstein's essay, 'Rediscovering Thomas Paine', for this delightful find, published in the *New York Law School Law Review*, Vol. XXXIX, No. 4, 1994.

FURTHER READING

The cornerstone work on Thomas Paine's life and writing was and remains that of the distinguished abolitionist and free-thinker Moncure Conway (after whom London's Conway Hall is named). His two-volume *Life of Thomas Paine* and his four-volume edition of *The Writings of Thomas Paine* were both published at the end of the nineteenth century but are still considered seminal.

The latter part of the last century saw a considerable revival in Paine studies. The best single volume biography is *Tom Paine: A Political Life*, by John Keane (1995) though I would also recommend Professor A. J. Ayer's *Thomas Paine* (1988). The Library of America produced an excellent two-volume *Collected Writings* in 1995.

For those principally interested in Paine's American aspect, there is *Thomas Paine's American Ideology*, by A. Owen Aldridge (1984) and *Thomas Paine and the Promise of America* by Harvey J. Kaye (2005). Paine's British admirers may like to consult the chapter on him in H. N. Brailsford's *Shelley, Godwin and Their Circle*, and Michael Foot's tribute in his collection *Debts of Honour*.

INDEX

3333

33

*Index compiled by Meg Davies
(Registered Indexer, Society of
Indexers)*